"This is simply the best book about the nature and function of the Bible that I have ever read! It is outstanding in describing the overall narrative of Scripture and in insisting that the individual 'bits' of the Bible are read in the context of that 'big picture.' It is outstanding in applying that same technique to people's lives. It is outstanding in the number of concrete examples he uses to illustrate his points. And it is outstanding most of all because it, like the Bible, clearly points to Jesus. Dr. Emlet has written a superb book, which anyone who wants to understand and apply the Bible really MUST read!"
SAMUEL T. LOGAN JR., Ph.D., International Director of the World Reformed Fellowship; theologian; author

"If you want to see how the gospel works in your life, transforming you by the renewing of the mind (the principle on which Jesus and the apostles 'fixed' broken lives) then here is a very good place to begin. Rather than offer you a prescription 'to get you through the next few weeks,' Dr. Emlet writes one that transforms deeply and lasts a whole lifetime."
SINCLAIR B. FERGUSON, Ph.D., Senior Minister, First Presbyterian Church, Columbia, S.C.; theologian; author of *The Christian Life*

"Depression. Divorce. Death of a loved one. Life can be messy, and pat 'Christian' answers won't help. That's why Mike Emlet wrote *CrossTalk*— to equip you to tackle real issues with practical, life-transforming truth from God's Word. If you want to enhance your clinical practice and learn how the Bible intimately connects with your clients' daily struggles, don't miss this book!"
DR. TIM CLINTON, President of the American Association of Christian Counselors; licensed therapist; author of *Turn Your Life Around*

"*CrossTalk* isn't your typical cut-and-paste counseling guide. No, it's deeper and richer than that. Its pages are filled with light, demonstrating a gloriously redemptive interpretation of Scripture and deep understanding of the condition and needs of the human heart. I highly recommend it."
ELYSE FITZPATRICK, Counselor, Institute for Biblical Counseling and Discipleship; author of *Women Helping Women*

"Ministry of the Word happens somewhere in between the proof-text snippet and the broad generalities of redemptive history. God's person, promises, purposes, actions, and commands catch fire in a person's struggle with personal sins and situational struggles. Mike Emlet probes for the places truth ignites and probes for the ways Christ indwells hearts and conversations."
DAVID POWLISON, Ph.D., Faculty and counselor at CCEF; author of *Seeing with New Eyes* and *Speaking Truth in Love*

"Mike Emlet's *CrossTalk* gives biblical counselors crucial lessons in applying the Scripture both accurately and wisely when working with broken and hurting people. Even seasoned counselors will find themselves challenged to dig harder into applying and living out the truths of God's Word."
LESLIE VERNICK, Speaker; counselor; author of *Lord, I Just Want to Be Happy*

"Rejecting widespread and simplistic ways of connecting Scripture to our lives, Emlet heads down a more faithful path. He offers helpful insight as well as concrete models that make the Bible come alive in the concrete details of human life. Anyone who wants to live more faithfully in the biblical story as well as help others to do so will benefit from reading this book."
MICHAEL W. GOHEEN, Ph.D., Geneva Professor of Worldview and Religious Studies, Trinity Western University; coauthor of *The Drama of Scripture*

"As a trained physician and now teacher and counselor, Emlet brings an immense wealth of knowledge and experience—helping us mine the whole counsel of God for the whole person. *CrossTalk* just moved to the top of my required reading list and is one I will commend to my parishioners to take and heed."
ALFRED POIRIER, D.Min., Author of *The Peacemaking Pastor*

"Thank you Michael Emlet for reminding us that we spend far too much time reducing the story of God's redemption to a digest version, rather than opening all of Scripture to connect it to people as saints, sufferers, and sinners."
ROD MAYS, D.Min., National Coordinator, Reformed University Ministries

"Here's a book I've been waiting for a long time: one that deals with the interpretation of the Bible for counseling. It is sophisticated in its understanding of the issues involved, but also practical and well within the reach of laypeople and counselors-in-training. Only two hundred pages, it is bigger than it looks. Its importance is evident in its grasp of the central message of Scripture—the story of Christ—and its instruction in how to use that story to help transform ours. Throughout, the spirit of the author comes across as a compassionate and biblical lover of souls."
ERIC JOHNSON, Ph.D., Professor of Pastoral Care, Southern Baptist Theological Seminary

"Michael Emlet's practical insights on bringing Scripture to bear on the challenging problems of life are both simple and powerful. Anyone who masters these principles and uses them in the love and grace of Christ, will be a channel of life-changing truth and wisdom into the lives of others. I thank God for this book and will recommend it to everyone I know."
KEN SANDE, President, Peacemaker Ministries; author of *The Peacemaker*

CrossTalk

Where Life & Scripture Meet

Michael R. Emlet

New
Growth
Press

www.newgrowthpress.com

New Growth Press, Greensboro, NC 27404

Cover Design: The DesignWorks Group, Nate Salciccioli and Jeff Miller, www.designworksgroup.com

Typesetting: Lisa Parnell

ISBN-13: 978-1-935273-12-7
ISBN-10: 1-935273-12-4

Library of Congress Cataloging-in-Publication Data

Emlet, Michael R.
  CrossTalk : where life & Scripture meet / Michael R. Emlet.
    p. cm.
  Includes bibliographical references and index.
  ISBN-13: 978-1-935273-12-7
  ISBN-10: 1-935273-12-4
  1. Christian life—Biblical teaching. 2. Bible—Use. I. Title.
  BS680.C47E46 2009
  220.07—dc22

                                                              2009022216

Printed in the United States of America

19 18 17 16 15 14 13 12   8 9 10 11 12

To Jody

With gratitude and joy

I'm privileged to wake up next to you each morning.

Contents

Acknowledgments

No one can write a book about the intersection of life and Scripture without a profound debt of gratitude to many people, past and present. I am acutely aware that I stand on the shoulders of giants.

Although I didn't fully grasp it at the time, the seeds of a redemptive-historical, Christ-centered approach to Scripture were consistently sown by Joe Novenson, my pastor in the early 1990s, in his preaching, teaching, and counseling. Through his mentoring and the encouragement of Tuck and Stacy Bartholomew, I came to Westminster Theological Seminary (Philadelphia) in 1996, blithely unaware of the Copernican revolution that was about to take place in my approach to Scripture and to people.

I am deeply thankful for the rich biblical-theological training I received from my professors at Westminster Theological Seminary, 1996–2001. Most particularly, Douglas Green and Richard B. Gaffin Jr. profoundly shaped my approach to the Scriptures of the Old and New Testaments.

Ed Welch, David Powlison, and Winston Smith have twice blessed me: by serving as my wise teachers during seminary and by welcoming me as their colleague at the Christian Counseling & Educational Foundation (CCEF), where I have been privileged to work since 2001. CCEF's biblically rooted approach to people and to the process of spiritual growth has profoundly benefited me, both personally and pastorally. My thanks to John Bettler, then executive director of CCEF, for bringing me on board. Tim Lane, current executive director of CCEF, has remained enthusiastic (and patient!) throughout this project. I am thankful for the gracious provision of a sabbatical in the spring of 2007 to begin in earnest the writing of this book.

The real impetus for writing on this subject has come from teaching a course each year on biblical interpretation at Westminster Theological Seminary. This course, taken mostly by counseling students, has served as the testing ground for many of the ideas in this book. My students have shown me that just when I think I have something "nailed down," they are able to ask a question that sends me scurrying back to the drawing board! I am thankful for their insights over the years. I had the privilege of coteaching the course with Bill Smith for several years and profited from his biblical wisdom and pastoral approach to people. My thanks also to Adrian Smith for lively, thoughtful conversations over coffee at the now defunct Phriends Café in Jenkintown, Pennsylvania, in the early years of teaching the course.

I have had many other conversation partners over the years. Jayne Clark, friend, colleague, and wise counselor, has consistently pointed me to Christ and is one who models what it means to "bring the Bible to life." David Powlison's thoughtful approach to the Bible as practical theology is foundational to this work. He is the epitome of one who connects—no, rivets(!)—Scripture to his own life. Steven Badorf, from the earliest days of our friendship in seminary to the present, has consistently pushed my approach to Scripture in thoughtful ways. Mike Kelly has been my teacher, colleague, elder, and close friend. I am especially grateful for many hours of conversations over the years regarding the intersection of biblical interpretation and personal ministry (among many other topics!).

Mari Stout and Adrian Smith read an early draft of the book and provided helpful feedback. Tuck Bartholomew, the organizing pastor of City Church Philadelphia, where my family and I are members, has been a wise and dear friend over many years. I have appreciated the opportunity to use some of the ideas of the book in our small-group leaders training.

I am grateful to have had several other opportunities to present this material, at various stages of development, outside the classroom: at the CCEF Annual Conference (November 2007) and at Christ Community Church, Chapel Hill, North Carolina (May 2008). I would like to thank the Society for Christian Psychology for the opportunity to do a preconference in September 2008; I appreciated Eric Johnson's kind invitation.

I am deeply grateful to Sue Lutz, who served as my editor. It's not an easy task to tackle an author's first book. She encouraged this project for many years before it ever took shape. I have appreciated both her careful editing and her wise approach to Scripture and people. She kept me from using too many polysyllabic words and consistently pushed me to take the material to the most concrete and pastoral of levels.

I am thankful for New Growth Press. I do not take lightly the opportunity that Karen and Mark Teears have offered me in publishing this book. I thank Karen, especially, for her enthusiasm and flexibility throughout a writing process that has taken longer than either of us anticipated. Thanks also to Barbara Juliani, editorial project manager at New Growth, who carefully shepherded the manuscript to publication.

My parents, Marvin and Miriam Emlet, have been warmly encouraging throughout my life. They never blinked an eye when I left medicine to pursue full-time ministry but welcomed this call of God. They, along with my sister Mileen, have undergirded this book with hours of prayer.

My gratitude to my family is more than words can say—but I'll try anyhow! My daughter Lydia and my son Luke are a delight to my heart. Perhaps more than anyone on earth, they have pushed me to practice what I preach. They eagerly anticipated the day when they could hold "Daddy's book" in their hands. I pray that they will continue to fall in love with the One to whom this book points. Finally, I dedicate this book to my wife Jody. Her love for God and for others grows out of the fact that she consistently lives by the redemptive plotline of Scripture. She knows Jesus— and it shows—every day. I am so thankful for the privilege of being her covenant companion for life.

Michael R. Emlet

Introduction

Rick sat in his chair, his eyes downcast. Despite a renewed commitment to Christ that was demonstrated in months of patient, self-sacrificial living at home, his wife of twenty-two years had decided to file for divorce. He looked up, furrowed his brow, and said, "What good was all this work to end up like this? I know God is up to something, but it feels like my efforts were in vain."

Max, his good friend and Bible study leader, responded, "Rick, I hardly know what to say. I know that this is deeply hurtful and disappointing to you." He sat in silence for a few moments then quietly said, "Your grief reminds me of the words of the Lord's servant in Isaiah 49:4: 'But I said, "I have labored to no purpose; I have spent my strength in vain and for nothing. Yet what is due me is in the LORD's hand, and my reward is with my God."'"

Rick looked up. "That really does describe how I feel. I know I need to take to heart the second part of that verse, but it's hard to have that perspective right now."

For the next two hours Rick and Max talked about dashed hopes and unfulfilled dreams, framing Rick's experience through a biblical lens. Ultimately they talked about Jesus, the true Servant of the Lord, who had every earthly reason to take Isaiah's lament upon his lips as he hung on the cross. Yet Jesus remained faithful, confident that he would be vindicated by his Father and that his reward lay with his God (Heb. 12:2; 1 Pet. 2:23). Although many

1

more late-night discussions would occur, Rick left that evening more confident that the words of the Servant could become his own.

Who wouldn't want the privilege of using Scripture to help someone in trouble, as Max did? How does that happen? If you're like me, you have probably received more instruction on how to study the Bible than you have on how to practically *use* it in your life and ministry. The fact is, there are many books about how to interpret the Bible, but most of these are heavy on the side of theory, not application, which is the spiritual task of connecting Scripture with life. These resources help us study the grammatical and literary details of a passage, do research into the original historical setting and audience, and draw some conclusions about what the passage might have meant to the original hearers/readers. All of this is valuable—in fact, it's absolutely essential. But the equally important step of relating that study to the messy complexity of life in the here and now is given relatively little attention, even in very good books on biblical interpretation. Too often, we remain people who are all messed up with no place to go!

Resources that focus more fully on the challenge of application tend to concentrate on public ministry such as preaching or teaching[1] or on broader questions of ethics in the life of the church.[2] But if we are asking how the Bible addresses the complexities of our personal lives (or another's life), there are fewer places to turn.

Of course, there is great overlap between using the Bible "macro-ethically" (e.g., applying its teaching to broader issues like divorce, urban blight, and homosexuality) and "micro-ethically" (e.g., learning to minister on a personal level to a friend struggling with the loss of a job or wrestling with anger). Broader issues always filter down to the level of personal decisions and actions, and personal issues always have a broader social context. The common concern is how the Bible should function ethically in our lives, whether one-on-one in personal ministry or in a larger church and cultural setting. In either case, we need a resource that helps connect the wisdom of Scripture with the details of our daily lives, a resource that helps us learn how to bridge the gap between then and now.

And now for a true confession: I wrote this book because *I* need this resource! As a biblical counselor who also trains other counselors, my daily challenge is to bring the good news of God's redemption to my counselees' lives—and to help others do the same. Questions (often from my students) frequently arise: "Why did you choose *that* passage?" "Why didn't you open your Bible that session?" "Why did you address that particular theme in this person's life?" "How could you be more gospel-centered with this brother?" "How do you build biblical hope for change in this sister?" These questions have prodded me to write about the process of connecting life and Scripture.

When we hit a personal "wall" in counseling or pastoral ministry, it provokes a more proactive, thoughtful approach to both people and the Bible. "How can I better understand this person biblically?" "*I* thought that Scripture was relevant; why didn't it connect with him?" "Why is this person 'stuck'?" "What biblical truth might help her grow?" All these questions from the trenches led me to investigate the intersection of biblical truth and peoples' lives—what is commonly referred to as "application."

The Focus of This Book

It might help you to know up front what this book will and will not cover. This book is not a comprehensive approach to biblical interpretation. It will not address in detail the interpretive process, but it will build on many of the concepts laid out in books that do. So, for example, I will not cover (in depth, at least) the guidelines for examining a passage in its original context, what biblical scholars call "grammatical-historical exegesis." I *will* mention several solid resources on biblical interpretation that can help if you have not received formal training in biblical interpretation. Similarly, I won't address how the varied literature types (genres) of the Bible—such as narrative, poetry, wisdom, prophecy, gospel, and epistle—impact the way you interpret and use Scripture.[3] Nor will I discuss the philosophical intricacies of where the meaning of a text comes from.[4]

Secondly, this book is not a comprehensive approach to discipleship, counseling, or pastoral care. It *does* provide a biblical "take" on people that I believe is foundational for personal ministry, but if you are looking for a book-length treatment on the nature of people and how to help them, this book probably will not address all your questions.[5]

Lastly, this book is not a survey of the major ethical challenges that confront the church today. I won't be discussing how to use the Bible to address issues such as homosexuality, global warming, women in ministry, and poverty, to name a few. No doubt, the way I propose that we understand the Bible, understand people, and understand the link between the two will impact our approach to "macro-ethical" issues. But my main focus is "micro-ethics"—how we use Scripture to meaningfully intersect with a *particular* person's life as we minister to him or her.

Consider this book a hybrid of sorts, a resource to help you understand both people and the Bible more thoroughly. This book gives attention to interpreting the biblical text and interpreting the person. Both skills are necessary if you are to minister in a way that correctly "handles the word of truth" (2 Tim. 2:15). Both are necessary for effective ministry.

To sum it up, this book can help you read the Bible and "read" people in a way that promotes gospel-centered, personally relevant use of Scripture in ministry to others. It describes a way to use the Scriptures to help people grow to love God and others more fully in the midst of their complex daily lives.

This Book's for You!

What kind of reader do I envision you to be? I'm hoping you are someone actively engaged in personal ministry—counselor, pastor, discipler, spiritual mentor, small-group leader, campus ministry worker, youth leader, crisis pregnancy worker, or intentional friend. I'm also hoping that you're someone who, like me, has wrestled with how to connect God's Word to the lives of people around you (and sometimes failed!). I hope you desire to see how two worlds fruitfully meet head-on: the unfolding story of God's redemption and the complex tapestries of peoples' struggles, sufferings, sin, triumphs, and joys.

If you are primarily involved in a more "public" ministry of the Word such as preaching and teaching, I believe the book will sharpen your approach to Scripture and to people. It's true that preaching and teaching tend to be more "proclamatory" in nature, whereas "private" ministry of the Word, which occurs one-on-one or in the context of small groups, tends to be more "dialogical" or conversational in nature. But whatever the sphere or scope of your work with others, I believe you will find help to grow in ministry wisdom.

Here's the bottom line: this book is for anyone who takes the "one another" passages of the Bible seriously and is eager to use the richness of Scripture to minister wisely to the people God has placed in his or her sphere of influence. It is for anyone who has been captured by Paul's vision for God's people, namely, "that the body of Christ may be built up until we all reach unity in the faith and in the knowledge of the Son of God and become mature, attaining to the whole measure of the fullness of Christ" (Eph. 4:12–13).

How Firm a Foundation

As we start exploring this topic, let's affirm two foundational truths about the Bible. These truths will support the weight of what follows in the rest of this book.

First, the Bible is God's "breathed-out" word, according to 2 Timothy 3:16a. Second Peter 1:20–21 notes, "Above all, you must understand that no prophecy of Scripture came about by the prophet's own interpretation. For prophecy never had its origin in the will of man, but men spoke from God as they were carried along by the Holy Spirit." Because the Bible is God's truthful word and not the flight of human fancy, it has authority (applicational weight) for God's people. It is, as Paul goes on to say, "useful for teaching, rebuking, correcting and training in righteousness" (2 Tim. 3:16b). Peter puts it this way: "His divine power has given us everything we need for life and godliness through our knowledge of him who called us by his own glory and goodness. Through these he has given us his very great and precious promises, so that through them you may participate in the divine nature and escape the corruption in the world caused by evil desires" (2 Pet. 1:3–4). Peter connects the knowledge of God, the Word (promises) of God, and our participation in God's nature or character. Both apostles would affirm that the Bible is a divinely authored means of God's grace to grow us into the likeness of Christ. God speaks to change us.

Second, God in his wisdom used human authors to bring his words to his people. The Bible did not drop out of the sky as a completed document, nor were the writers of Scripture mindless drones who merely took dictation from God. Rather, in some mysterious divine-human collaboration, the human writers of Scripture wrote words that were truly their own, yet simultaneously the exact words that God the Holy Spirit intended, specifically tailored for God's people living within a certain historical and cultural moment.[6] Jeannine Brown connects these two aspects of Scripture by describing the Bible as "culturally located divine discourse."[7] Keeping this balance reminds us that (1) God revealed himself progressively in history through the Bible's human authors *and* (2) the Bible, because God is the ultimate author, remains authoritative for his people throughout all time.

The Story of God and the Stories of People

From what I have just said, it is clear that God's Word is meant to *inform* and *transform* God's people. How God's redemptive message does that is the focus of this book. But for now, realize that the Bible proclaims one comprehensive true story of God's relationship with people. It moves from creation to the fall of humanity into sin, suffering, and death, to redemption—ultimately accomplished through Jesus—and finally, to a vision of God's kingdom, complete at Jesus' second coming.[8] It is the story of God creating a people to rule the world on his behalf, for their good and his glory. It is a story of their rebellion against God's wise design. But it is also a tale of God rescuing his people from their sin and misery, and the climax of that narrative comes in the life, death, and resurrection of Jesus the Messiah.

Everything in the Old Testament looks forward to this climax and everything in the New Testament looks back to it and/or works out its implications for the lives of God's people. Of course, the New Testament also looks *forward* to Jesus' second coming. This is what the gospel is all about: the good news that God entered history as the man Jesus to bring about the redemption of a people and a world bound in sin and suffering.

But not "generic" redemption. Not "generic" sin and suffering. This good news reaches God's people in the trenches of life and is tailored to the particularities of life. Any attempts at ministering God's Word that do not fundamentally connect the good news of the Redeemer, Jesus Christ, with the details, themes, and plotlines of people's lives will miss the mark (or land off the target altogether!). Hence, it is appropriate to call the approach of this book "redemptive-historical"[9] or "gospel-centered" application. It is an approach that takes the narrative (storied) nature of the Bible seriously in order to make wise connections with the narratives of our lives. Understanding both the Story of God and the stories of the people we serve is necessary to help others embrace the transformation the Bible envisions for God's people.

The Goals of This Book

What specific goals do I have in mind for this book? What do I hope to see happen in your life as a result of reading it? The first goal has to do with your own relationship with God. The apostle John wrote, "these [things] are written that you may believe that Jesus is the Christ, the Son of God, and that by believing you may have life in his name" (John 20:31). That life does not begin in some future place following death. It starts right here, right now, as God brings restoration into the midst of a broken creation (2 Cor. 5:17). God intends our lives to reflect the life of Christ as we encounter him through his Word (2 Pet. 1:4). So, one goal for this book is that your life would be increasingly shaped and transformed by the sweeping story of Scripture. As Eugene Peterson says, "If Holy Scripture is to be something other than mere gossip about God, it must be internalized."[10]

A temptation in ministry is to think that just because we prepared for a Bible study, a sermon, or a discipleship appointment (or wrote a book like this!), we are deeply engaging with the God of the universe. But that's not necessarily true. It's easy in ministry to live more as a "pipe" than a "reservoir." That is, it's easy to live merely as a conduit to others of the transforming truths of God's Word, rather than as a changed and transformed reservoir who overflows with lived-out gospel truth. You wouldn't imagine cooking meal after meal for your family without sitting down to enjoy that nourishment yourself, would you? To paraphrase James 1:22, let's not merely be hearers or speakers or counselors of the Word but doers, first and foremost.

A second goal relates to your relationships with others. If you want to speak helpfully to a struggling brother or sister, this book should increase your ability to listen, ask thoughtful questions, and use biblical categories for interpreting their experiences. Perhaps you have been in a situation where someone asked for your input on a matter. But when you tried to bring biblical truth to the table, it felt as though you were changing the subject (at least from the other person's perspective)! This book should help you interpret people as well as Scripture and suggest relevant biblical applications that will benefit those around you. This should be true whether you are involved in a formal teaching or discipling ministry, in professional counseling, or in impromptu discussions at the local café.

A third goal relates to your attitude toward the Bible and the way you use it in ministry. As you grow to appreciate the unified story line of the Bible *as well as* the uniqueness of individual books and passages, I hope that your Bible will "grow" in size. That is, I hope you will see the wonder and beauty of the gospel in whatever Old or New Testament passage you are reading. This should encourage you to dive into portions of the Bible you previously neglected. It should motivate you to explore the way these passages relate to Jesus Christ—and how they relate to your own situations in life and ministry.

Put simply, the overall goal of this book is to help you live a biblically rich, Christ-centered life in community with fellow believers. It will equip you to make more sense of the details of the Bible and the details of people's lives. It will equip you to see how the diverse writings of Scripture have a cohesive, kingdom-centered thrust. And it will help you discern life patterns, themes, and plotlines that underlie the details of people's experiences. Ultimately, it should equip you to more carefully read the story of the Bible and the diverse stories of the people you know and to make meaningful connections between the two.

The title *CrossTalk: Where Life & Scripture Meet* captures several of these ideas in overlapping ways. First, *CrossTalk* highlights the interpersonal aspect of ministry and carries the idea of redemptive dialogue occurring between two or more people. Second, the title emphasizes the centrality of the gospel. It highlights personal ministry that points to the Redeemer, Jesus Christ—his life, death on the cross, resurrection, ascension, and future return. Finally, *CrossTalk* focuses our attention on the intersection of two kinds of "speech"—the story of Scripture and the stories of people's lives. This is the place of application. This is *CrossTalk* in action.

Let's begin by exploring the real challenges of connecting the Bible to life.

Discussion Questions

1. What questions and struggles do you have in applying Scripture to life?
2. Describe your current method of studying and interpreting Scripture.
3. Describe your current approach to understanding and interpreting people.
4. How have you seen your study of Scripture specifically lead to a changed life—your own or another's?

CHAPTER 1

Connecting
the Bible to Life

Do you find it easy or difficult to connect the Bible to people's lives in meaningful ways? To help you answer the question, let me give you a quiz of sorts for some self-evaluation.

I will give you two sets of questions: one on Bible Passages and the other on Life Struggles. For the Bible Passages category, you must think of a contemporary life situation to which you could apply the given passage. For the Life Struggles category, you must choose a Bible passage you believe would address the problem. Each question may have several "correct" answers. Answer each question before reading the succeeding paragraph. (You're on the honor system!)

Let's start with Bible Passages.

1. "Do not be anxious about anything, but in everything, by prayer and petition, with thanksgiving, present your requests to God" (Phil. 4:6).

    More than likely, you thought of situations such as the following: "trusting in God to overcome worry in a financial crisis," "dealing with a loved one's impending death," "facing final exams," "giving your first sermon series," "doing beach evangelism on a summer missions project." What do these answers have in common? They are all situations that can provoke anxiety or worry, right? The passage appears to speak about how to handle worry so, naturally, anxiety-producing situations come to mind as places for potential application.

2. The Story of Joseph (Gen. 37—50)

Perhaps situations like these came to mind: "how to respond in a godly way when fired unjustly from your job," "persevering in hope when facing persecution from non-Christians," "maintaining a perspective that God is working out his purposes even in a series of setbacks, like the ending of a two-year relationship or a pay cut at work." The way you answered this question depends on what you think the story of Joseph is about and how much you used Joseph's experience and character in your application.

3. The Philistines capture the ark of the covenant (1 Sam. 4).

This passage may be less familiar to you. For that reason alone, potential applications may not easily come to mind. But if you read the passage, does *anything* come to mind? Unlike the Joseph story, there are no characters to emulate. (You definitely don't want to be a Hophni or Phinehas!) Unlike the Joseph narrative, there appears to be no happy ending. Here is a passage where the ark, the dwelling place of God, gets captured by Israel's archenemy. The glory has departed! How "applicable" is this, really? And should it be applied in isolation from what happens in chapters 3 and 5?

4. "Alexander the metalworker did me a great deal of harm. The Lord will repay him for what he has done. You too should be on your guard against him, because he strongly opposed our message" (2 Tim. 4:14–15).

If your first thought was, *Huh?!* that's quite appropriate! (If your response was, "Watch out for angry atheist welders," you get extra points for creativity!) Seriously, what should you do with a passage like this? Can you really apply it to a contemporary life situation? If you were able to come up with a potential application, what interpretive "moves" allowed you to generate that application? *Should* it be that easy?

Now let's move to the Life Struggles category. For each problem or situation below, consider what biblical passages might apply.

1. Anger

   You may have chosen passages such as the following: "'In your anger do not sin': Do not let the sun go down while you are still angry, and do not give the devil a foothold" (Eph. 4:26–27); "My dear brothers, take note of this: Everyone should be quick to listen, slow to speak and slow to become angry, for man's anger does not bring about the righteous life that God desires" (James 1:19–20); "A gentle answer turns away wrath, but a harsh word stirs up anger" (Prov. 15:1). Much like the first question in the Bible Passages category, this seems easy, right? In all likelihood, the passages that came to your mind mention anger in some way and, I would bet, are command-oriented. But did you consider the story of Cain and Abel? Isn't that a story of anger? What about the many Old Testament passages that talk about *God's* anger? Could you have chosen one of them? And didn't Jesus get angry with the Pharisees? Finally, is it ever appropriate to choose a passage that doesn't explicitly speak about anger to help an angry person?

2. Conflict in Relationships

   How about this? "What causes fights and quarrels among you? Don't they come from your desires that battle within you? You want something but don't get it. You kill and covet, but you cannot have what you want. You quarrel and fight. You do not have, because you do not ask God. When you ask, you do not receive, because you ask with wrong motives, that you may spend what you get on your pleasures" (James 4:1–3); or "Don't have anything to do with foolish and stupid arguments, because you know they produce quarrels. And the Lord's servant must not quarrel; instead, he must be kind to everyone, able to teach, not resentful" (2 Tim. 2:23–24); or possibly, "Let the peace of Christ rule in your hearts, since as members of one body you were called to peace. And be thankful" (Col. 3:15). Again, it's not too difficult to generate a list of passages that are fairly direct in their treatment of conflict.

3. An infertile couple wants to know what technology is biblically permissible to use to achieve pregnancy.

Not so easy, right? No single passage of Scripture comes to mind quickly, I would suspect. With more thought, you might consider Paul's response to the Corinthians, who were testing the bounds of Christian liberty: "'Everything is permissible for me'—but not everything is beneficial. 'Everything is permissible for me'—but I will not be mastered by anything" (1 Cor. 6:12). OK, but do you realize that Paul is focusing on sexual immorality in this passage? Is it appropriate to apply it to such a different problem? Or would you go to Psalm 139 and build a case that life begins at conception, as a guard against the creation of multiple embryos? Or is there something more important in order to minister the gospel wisely and compassionately to this couple?

4. A gambling addict with bipolar disorder, now taking three different psychoactive medications, has a daughter who just attempted suicide.

Let me save you some time. The most appropriate answer here is Job's response: "I am unworthy—how can I reply to you? I put my hand over my mouth. I spoke once, but I have no answer— twice, but I will say no more" (40:4–5). In other words, this is too complex to solve with an easy appeal to the Bible. This is not to say that Scripture is irrelevant to this man's struggle. Quite the contrary! But it's important to realize that the ease of considering the relevant testimony of Scripture has declined significantly from our first example.

Now, let's go back to my initial question: Is it easy or difficult to connect the Bible and life? It depends, doesn't it? I'm going to call what you just experienced the "Ditch vs. Canyon Phenomenon."

What I mean is this: sometimes use of Scripture in ministry has the feel of stepping across a ditch (easy!), and sometimes it has the feel of stepping across a canyon (impossible!). The challenge, really, is how to bridge the gap between an ancient biblical text and a present-day life situation. How do we attempt to bridge that divide? Most of the time we assume that a direct line of connection must exist between the situation then (in the text) and the situation now. Or at the very least we think we can extract some "timeless principle" from the text and bring it to the present. This mind-set, where we assume some kind of one-to-one correspondence between a text then and a situation now, is admirable in its goal to "make" the Scriptures relevant for the believer today.

And, in fact, it often works when the passage speaks specifically about a situation or experience we're facing. Here are some examples of "ditch" passages. If you're not familiar with these passages, look them up as you go and see if you agree.

- Psalm 23 for fear
- Psalm 51 for repentance
- Proverbs 22:15 for disciplining a child
- Matthew 5:27–30 for understanding the depth and breadth of adultery/sexual lust
- Ephesians 5:22–33 for marriage roles and relationships
- Philippians 4:6 for anxiety (as mentioned earlier) along with Ephesians, James, and Proverbs passages on anger

Other passages seem to fit in this category, but they stretch the width of the ditch a bit more. What I mean is, these passages might not speak as specifically and explicitly about a particular struggle or situation, but they seem "close enough" to allow for a relatively quick connection. Sometimes it's because of the positive or negative example the passage provides, and sometimes it's because of a general principle derived from the text. All in all, the path to application still feels relatively direct. For example:

- Numbers 11 as a warning against grumbling and complaining about your job

- Philippians 4:8 for training your mind against sexually lustful thoughts
- Joshua 1:9 as encouragement as you begin an evangelistic crusade in your church
- The story of Joseph as an encouragement amid harassment or persecution from others

But looking for the more direct connection ends up backfiring when we encounter passages that seem far removed from our day-to-day experiences. For example, when was the last time we demolished a house because of a mildew problem (Lev. 14:33–57)? Or used Numbers 5:11–31 as a test for adultery for couples in our congregations?[1] When have we used the regulations for the building of the tabernacle (Exod. 25—31; 35—40) to encourage someone? What life-changing application have we made lately from the first nine chapters of 1 Chronicles, which is essentially a list of names? What should we do with Obadiah (a prophecy against Edom)? When have we used Revelation 17 (the woman and the beast) in a counseling session? What should we do with very specifically directed passages, as noted earlier with Alexander the metalworker in 2 Timothy? Suddenly we find ourselves facing a canyon! Now what?

Our tendency, of course, is to gravitate toward the "ditch" passages because they seem easier to apply; it's easier to make a connection between then and now. Ditch passages resonate more quickly with our experiences. They have a greater immediacy, so we hang out in these tried-and-true passages and we skim—or avoid altogether—those pesky canyon passages. But what is the result?

In practical terms, we end up ministering with an embarrassingly thinner but supposedly more relevant Bible. Did you ever wonder why publishers sell the New Testament packaged together with Psalms and Proverbs?[2] Why not sell the New Testament with Leviticus and Esther? Or the New Testament with 1 and 2 Kings and the Minor Prophets? A value judgment is being made. The New Testament, Psalms, and Proverbs are deemed more relevant for contemporary life. The New Testament is included because it's about Jesus and the church. Proverbs makes the grade because of all that pithy, helpful, concrete advice. And the Psalms are important because of the emotions they evoke and because of their use in worship. (Of course, one must overlook the difficulties of using, for example, Psalm 3:7 in a ministry situation: "Arise O LORD! Deliver me, O my God! Strike all my enemies on the jaw; break the teeth of the wicked.")

Have you succumbed to this mind-set even if you don't frequently use an "abridged" Bible? Take a look at the Bible you regularly use—which pages are the dirtiest and most dog-eared? Hmm. The hard reality is this: genealogies, dietary laws, battle records, and prophecies against ancient nations all take a backseat to parts of the Bible that connect more easily and naturally to our modern lives. And this is true despite believing that *all* of Scripture is "God-breathed" and "useful for teaching, rebuking, correcting and training in righteousness" (2 Tim. 3:16). We confess that all of Scripture is helpful for all of life, but that's not the way the Bible actually functions in our lives and ministries.

The challenge is not just in moving from the Bible to everyday life but also in moving from present-day problems to the Scriptures. Many modern-day struggles and problems don't seem to be addressed in the Scriptures; there seems to be no point in exploring the biblical world for guidance. We are confident that the Bible speaks relevantly and authoritatively to ditch problems, the everyday issues we all experience, such as anger, conflict, pride, fear, and money. It's easy to think of a passage (or passages) that deals with those life problems, right? You experienced this earlier when you took the quiz.

But where would you turn in Scripture to address anorexia and bulimia? Or (as we saw) the challenge of infertility? Should you counsel Mr. and Mrs. Jensen to separate in the midst of their troubled marriage? Should Christian parents homeschool or send their children to Christian schools or to public schools? Is it OK to place your children in day care so you can work? How do you help someone who obsesses about the contamination of objects around her and washes her hands repeatedly, to the point of bleeding? What does the Bible say about helping a child diagnosed with Asperger syndrome? Or a person diagnosed with bipolar disorder? The list is infinite!

If you have a passage that you think quickly captures any one of these issues fully, I would almost guarantee that your hearer will find it superficial or irrelevant.[3] The direct approach doesn't seem to work with these canyon problems. But if the Bible becomes functionally irrelevant, people will turn elsewhere for guidance on these thorny questions and issues.

Widened Ditches and Narrowed Canyons

Before I muddy the waters a bit regarding the ease with which we use ditch passages, let me affirm several things. First, it's absolutely right to use passages that speak specifically to our everyday experiences. As believers in Christ, we have continuity with God's people in the Old Testament and New Testament. We share the same struggles common to people of all eras, so we should expect God's revelation to *them* to resonate with *us.* In addition, let's not forget that God's Spirit gives wisdom and direction in the application of Scripture to life. Although I will stress throughout this book the importance of deeper study of Scripture and people, I want to affirm the often impromptu, Spirit-led connections between the Bible and life that you have experienced in ministry. You already have the mind of Christ (1 Cor. 2:16). At the same time, just because God's Spirit graciously uses your current knowledge of Scripture to connect with people, that doesn't mean you shouldn't dig deeper as you have opportunity. View this book, then, as an opportunity to dig for more treasure, even as you use and enjoy the riches you already have found!

So grab a shovel and consider this challenge: *Should* ditch passages be so easy to apply? Consider one of the easiest of ditch passages, Philippians 4:6–7: "Do not be anxious about anything, but in everything, by prayer and petition, with thanksgiving, present your requests to God. And the peace of God, which transcends all understanding, will guard your hearts and your minds in Christ Jesus." Have you used that passage in your own life and ministry in the midst of fear, anxiety, and worry? I certainly have. My concern is not whether this is a helpful passage to use in this situation—it is! Rather, my concern is *how* we go about using it and whether we have at least considered some of the complexities surrounding the use of this "easy" passage.

For example, has it ever hit you that there is about a two-thousand-year gap between the Philippians who received Paul's letter and your friend who is struggling with anxiety? How much overlap is there between the people, the social-cultural context, and situation(s) in that first-century church and suburban America two millennia later? More fundamentally, how can a snippet of ancient mail addressed to other people bear fruit in our lives today? Of course, one answer is, because it's in the Bible, it is God's revelation for believers of all ages, times, and places. That is true! At the same time, I don't want us to sidestep the historical, cultural, and situational gap that exists between the first century and now. What gives us the right to extract a verse or two and import it to the present without giving attention to its original context? Shouldn't we take that into consideration?

As I'm writing this, the Republican and Democratic races for the 2008 presidential election are in full swing. One tactic used time and time again during the debates is for one candidate to seize upon a phrase or statement of an opponent, rip it out of its context, and use it to characterize (caricature) the opponent's position. We chafe at such misrepresentation in politics or in our own relationships and conversations.

That is why we need to ask a question we often cheerfully ignore: How can we be so sure we are using Scripture properly when we apply it to our friends' situations? How can we be sure we are doing justice to the author's intent? Put another way, how can we judge if we have successfully traveled to the first century and back again with the apostle's meaning intact?

That challenge is even greater when we consider Old Testament passages. Is it fair to use Joshua 1:9 as an encouragement for an evangelistic campaign without considering the historical and cultural gap between then and now?[4] What do nomadic Israelites about to engage in bloody warfare have to do with fearful believers about to share tracts with drug users on the streets of north Philadelphia? Suddenly, ditches look more like canyons!

Similarly, life problems aren't as easy to assign to the ditch category. The fact is, people's lives are a complex maze of thoughts, emotions, actions, motives, circumstances, and experiences. What do you say to the angry wife who lives with a lazy, irresponsible alcoholic and is trying to deal with four children in various states of anger and rebellion themselves? Should you take her to Ephesians 4 to instruct her regarding her anger? Maybe. But maybe not.

Or consider how God's Word ministers to the man who cannot rid himself of the anxious thought that he left the door unlocked when he left for work that morning. How does scriptural truth interrupt his cycle of obsessive thinking and the compulsive checking that disrupts his schedule every day? Will you take him to Philippians 4:6–7 or Matthew 6:25–34, which speak explicitly about worry? Perhaps. But perhaps not. Is, in fact, a passage on worry most apropos? Are you sure that's the most important pastoral issue to address?

We need to realize that so-called ditch passages and ditch problems may not be so straightforward after all. *Great,* you may be thinking, *You've just taken my already 'small' functional Bible and made it even smaller! Now I feel even* more *tentative about using Scripture in ministry!* If you feel that way, please read again the first paragraph of this section! I do not want to make it more difficult for you to minister to others using the Bible. My intent is not to open a Pandora's box of difficulties that limit your application of Scripture. Rather, I hope you will sense increasing freedom in your ministry as you engage the Bible and people more deeply. What might this look like?

I learned to play tennis in high school. I received minimal instruction but played frequently, so I became a decent player. Years later I played for the first time with a friend who had been a standout on his collegiate team. He asked if I wanted some pointers. He recognized that I had nearly reached the limits of my previous instruction and practice. We started with my serve. Suddenly the racket felt like a foreign object in my hand! Double fault after double fault ensued. I seemed to regress rather than progress. But, over time, what initially felt awkward became smoother and more skillful. Eventually, my new style of serving surpassed the accuracy, speed, and spin of the old. There was a long-term payoff. In a similar way, I don't want to take away your well-practiced "service" of ditch passages; I want to help you make it even better!

Consider the challenges I have posed so far as "speed bumps," particularly for the use of ditch passages for ditch problems. Slow down! There's more than meets the eye for this passage or this person. Seek to deepen your Spirit-led intuitions, and your use of Scripture will be even more fruitful. Your "hunches" with Scripture and with people may be right on target, but how much more helpful your ministry will be when you understand them even more deeply from the Christ-centered perspective this book advocates.

Let me give further encouragement: canyon passages aren't so impossible and canyon problems aren't so impossible! What makes canyon passages such as the building of the tabernacle, the book of Obadiah, or 1 Chronicles 1—9 potentially meaningful for believers today is that they are all part of an unfolding story of God's redemption, a redemption that finds its climax in Jesus Christ and into which we've been caught up by God's magnificent grace.[5] We are those "on whom the fulfillment of the ages has come" (1 Cor. 10:11). Because we are united with the One who fulfills (completes) Israel's story, we share some measure of continuity with the Old Testament people of God, on whose behalf Exodus or Obadiah or Chronicles was written. Similarly, we stand after the cross, resurrection, and the pouring out of the Spirit, in continuity with the New Testament writers and their audiences. What sets up Philemon or the most perplexing parts of Revelation (or any part of the New Testament) to be relevant for us today is that we share the same Savior, the same redemption, and the renewed kingdom brought by Jesus Christ.

It is true that the Bible is historically and culturally situated. And it's true that those factors require careful consideration in our interpretive efforts, a fact I will stress throughout this book. But because the Bible is "divine discourse"[6] that finds its fulfillment in *the* Word, Jesus Christ, we will find that *he* is the key for bridging canyons (or ditches for that matter). It's *our* Book because it's *his* Book, and we are his!

What about canyon problems? Although the Bible does not give an exhaustive, step-by-step approach to modern problems unforeseen by the biblical writers, it does provide a comprehensive view of people and problems that allows us to wisely dive into the thorniest issues of contemporary life. It treats sin and suffering in such profound and multifaceted ways that no struggle, no matter how complex, stands outside the gospel light it sheds. It is wisdom that unravels the Gordian knots of twenty-first-century struggles.

I hope this book will help you discover that your tried-and-true ditch passages are richer, deeper, and more challenging than you ever dared imagine; and that you will find canyon passages much more alive and accessible. At the same time, I hope you will discover that ditch problems are more complex than at first glance, and that canyon problems are somewhat demystified with a consistent biblical approach for understanding people. In short, I hope you will gain a nuanced approach to the Bible *and* to people that will lead to even more fruitful ministry.

To get there, we need to begin with the nature of the Bible itself. What exactly *is* this Book upon which we stake our lives and ministry? How do we recover the whole Bible for the whole of life? That is our journey over the next two chapters.

Discussion Questions

1. Which verses, passages, or books of the Bible do you tend to return to again and again? Why?
2. Are there parts of the Bible you have never read? Why?
3. What current problems in your life, ministry, and church community defy an easy application of Scripture? How are you seeking to bring God's Word to bear on those struggles?

CHAPTER 2
What the Bible Is Not
(Primarily)

I enjoy shopping at Home Depot or Lowe's, but it can be overwhelming. All the tools, hardware, and appliances dazzle me, but I'm not very mechanically minded. Many of the items would sit uselessly in my basement were I to buy them. Why? Because to use a tool wisely, you need to know what it is and what it does.

The same is true in ministry. We hold in our hands God's amazing personal revelation to us. We know the Bible reveals his character and redemptive purposes. We know that through it the Spirit of Jesus brings life. We have seen ourselves (and others) transformed by its practical truth. But do we ever stop to ask whether we are using the Bible in a way that maximizes its Christ-centered message? Do we ever pause to consider, "What *is* the Bible anyway? What kind of book did God give us? And what does this mean for the way we use it in ministry?" If we're honest, we have to admit that we sometimes find a disconnect between what we believe the Bible is and how we actually use it in real life.

The purpose of the next two chapters is to affirm the essential nature of the Scriptures because this affirmation must precede any interpretation and application we do. What the Bible primarily *is* determines how we ought to interpret and apply it.

This should not surprise us. We go through this process every time we encounter a text. What we expect to learn and how we anticipate using the material varies based on the nature of the written document before us. For example, your interpretive approach to the owner's manual for your car will differ from your approach to your daughter's e-mail. The way you read the editorial page of the newspaper will be different from the way you read the business section, because you implicitly recognize that the nature of these texts are different and therefore demand a different interpretive attitude. You recognize that the editorial page showcases the writer's opinions, while the business section contains a more straightforward reporting of events. Because of this, you are likely to use the information from both sources in different ways. Similarly, your approach to an article in the *New York Times* will be vastly different from your approach to a piece from the *National Enquirer* (at least I hope so!).

Even the way we interpret individual statements will vary based on the type of literature in which they appear. The caption "Tigers Devour Cubs in Record Time" will evoke one interpretation if you're reading about a fast-paced baseball game on the sports page. But it will bring a different response if you are reading a *National Geographic* account of predatory life in the wild!

That is why it is crucial to begin with this beguilingly simple question. The nature of the Bible—what the Bible is—must shape the way we interpret and apply it. In fact, when we see it clearly, the nature of the Bible is what supplies the rationale to do application in the first place! That is, the Bible's identity and character are what supply the answers to the questions, "How do we know the Bible is meant for us today? What gives us the right to use ancient documents originally meant for other people? How should we apply this revelation to our lives?" So, what *is* the Bible anyway, this collection of books from Genesis to Revelation?

Let's begin with some affirmations about what the Bible primarily is *not* because I think the following views of Scripture are fairly entrenched in our evangelical culture. Though each of these positions has merit, none, individually or together, captures the essential nature and purpose of the Scriptures. What's more, each affirmation, as you will see, leads to an approach to application that is shortsighted or deficient in some way.[1] By seeing the short-comings of each view, you will be in a better position to use the Scriptures to help struggling people.

The Bible Is *Not* Primarily a Book of Do's and Don'ts

This view of Scripture rightly recognizes that commands, exhortations, and prohibitions are throughout the Bible. God expects and commands a response from his people! As Jesus says, "Whoever has my commands and obeys them, he is the one who loves me" (John 14:21). Obedience matters, and that obedience has very specific contours. God's self-revelation is meant to regulate and shape the details of our lives. Loving God with heart, soul, and strength (Deut. 6:5) is not left hanging as a generic command. God fleshes it out for his people in many specific ways. We see it in the laws God gave Moses on Mount Sinai. We witness it in the exhortations of the prophets to backsliding Israel. We notice it in the words of Jesus. We experience it in the specific commands Paul gave to various churches. The Bible does provide norms for life. This is all true, but several problems arise with using the Bible *principally* as a kind of "rule book" for life.

First, large chunks of Scripture in both the Old and New Testaments have a relatively small proportion of imperatives or commands. Much of Scripture seems to be *descriptive* rather than obviously *prescriptive*. Much of Scripture doesn't tell us to do anything at all, particularly the historically oriented books. Do these books nonetheless provide guidelines for obedience? This is one reason why we gravitate to passages that contain commands. It seems easier to determine what we are to *do* after studying the verse or passage. This is particularly crucial when people seek our counsel. The stakes are high. Surely we want neither to add to nor subtract from what God asks of believers.

But this leads to a second issue: If we are law-oriented, how do we decide which rules apply in our contemporary situation and which rules do not?[2] For example, consider the following commands:[3]

- "Be fruitful and increase in number; fill the earth and subdue it. Rule over the fish of the sea and the birds of the air and over every living creature that moves on the ground" (Gen. 1:28).
- "You shall have no other gods before me" (Exod. 20:3).
- "Do not steal. Do not lie. Do not deceive one another" (Lev. 19:11).
- "Do not wear clothing woven of two kinds of material" (Lev. 19:19c).
- "If a man has a stubborn and rebellious son who does not obey his father and mother and will not listen to them when they discipline him, his father and mother shall take hold of him and bring him to the elders at the gate of his town. They shall say to the elders, 'This son of ours is stubborn and rebellious. He will not obey us. He is a profligate and a drunkard.' Then all the men of his town shall stone him to death. You must purge the evil from among you" (Deut. 21:18–21).
- "Do not withhold good from those who deserve it, when it is in your power to act" (Prov. 3:27).
- "Learn to do right! Seek justice, encourage the oppressed. Defend the cause of the fatherless, plead the case of the widow" (Isa. 1:17).
- "Do not store up for yourselves treasures on earth, where moth and rust destroy, and where thieves break in and steal" (Matt. 6:19).
- "Slaves, obey your earthly masters with respect and fear, and with sincerity of heart, just as you would obey Christ" (Eph. 6:5).
- "And one thing more: Prepare a guest room for me, because I hope to be restored to you in answer to your prayers" (Philemon 22).

Why would we have the impulse to keep Leviticus 19:11 but scrap Leviticus 19:19? Why don't we administer capital punishment for rebellious teens according to Deuteronomy? You might say that the situation of Israel as a theocracy, with the death sentence in place for certain forms of disobedience, is no longer relevant for our context. More broadly, you might maintain that specific people (e.g., Paul) give some commands to specific people (e.g., Philemon) in specific, historical situations (e.g., the case of Onesimus, Philemon's runaway slave). Fair enough! But isn't that true of every command listed above? Coming up with an acceptable set of applicable rules may not be so easy after all.

Consider what might be the most universal of the commands listed above, the imperative to "have no other gods before me," the first of the Ten Commandments. But even the Ten Commandments were given by specific persons (God, through Moses) to specific people (the Israelites) in a specific, nontransferable context (the rescue of the Israelites from their slavery in Egypt).[4]

To be sure, the first of the Ten Commandments itself, separated from its context, seems more relevant or universal than Paul's directive to Philemon, but that's another problem with the rule-book view of the Bible: namely, that this view of Scripture "decontextualizes" the Bible. It views commands as isolated entities, detached from the real, flesh-and-blood, historical situations that prompted the commands in the first place. We never communicate in this atomistic way as human beings! If meaningful communication occurs, it is because our words are spoken into the shared contexts and assumptions of the speaker and listener.

Third, even among commands considered relevant, an "importance hierarchy" of sorts will develop. Certain traditions may emphasize commands having to do with social justice. Others may choose to emphasize commands regarding evangelism or purity of doctrine. Isn't there some overarching understanding of Scripture that can keep us from focusing on certain commands to the exclusion of others?

If the Bible is essentially a book of commands, what gives us the right to pick and choose which ones apply now?[5] We need something beyond the individual commands themselves, an interpretive approach (supplied by the Bible itself) that puts those commands in a broader redemptive or relational framework. Only then will the full import and relevance of the commands and prohibitions come to light for us today.

Lastly, an exclusive focus on commands paradoxically may minimize the God who graciously redeems us. As we'll see in only a minute, the Bible never separates imperatives from their basis in God's redeeming love. To create a wedge between the two is a recipe for discouragement and ultimately strips the gospel of its power for change.

Many years ago in medical practice, before I went to seminary, I referred a patient for counseling because of a sexual addiction. He was a professing believer but could not seem to escape years of entrenched sexual lust. Despite many conversations he never gained much traction. The Christian counselor heard his story, then proceeded to instruct him to write Philippians 4:8 on an index card: "Finally, brothers, whatever is true, whatever is noble, whatever is right, whatever is pure, whatever is lovely, whatever is admirable—if anything is excellent or praiseworthy—think about such things." The counselor told him to keep the index card with him at all times and to pull it out of his pocket to read when sexual temptation came. This was to serve as a reminder of what he should be thinking about.

A few weeks later my patient returned to me, more discouraged than ever. His counselor had not served him well. He had so focused on the content of the command that he had neglected the gracious redemptive work of God that is the basis and motivation for keeping the command in the first place. My patient needed to see more clearly the God who pursues him in love, who gives commands that ultimately free his people to live as they were created to live.

Similarly, to use a parenting analogy, consider what happens when you give your child a command. Sometimes the child responds, "Why?" This *may* represent resistance to obedience, but it may also simply reflect a plea to understand the reason behind the command. The irritated parental response, "Because I said so," does not engender wholehearted obedience! Rather, children who understand their God-given place in the family, the love of their parents, and God's love for them will be in a better place to hear instruction and obey.

These examples highlight the fact that the commands of Scripture are always relationally rooted.[6] God rescues his people and then he says, "Now live in the freedom of my redemption in these specific ways." Often that relational foundation immediately precedes or follows the command. Here are several brief examples. As you read them, consider the way the relational basis for the command impacts the way you hear and understand it.

- "Do nothing out of selfish ambition or vain conceit, but in humility consider others better than yourselves. Each of you should look not only to your own interests, but also to the interests of others" (Phil. 2:3–4). Here is what precedes it: "If you have any encouragement from being united with Christ, if any comfort from his love, if any fellowship with the Spirit, if any tenderness and compassion . . ." (Phil. 2:1).
- "Set your hearts on things above, where Christ is seated at the right hand of God. Set your minds on things above, not on earthly things" (Col. 3:1b–2). Notice the rationale that precedes and follows: "Since, then, you have been raised with Christ . . ." (Col. 3:1a) and "For you died, and your life is now hidden with Christ in God. When Christ, who is your life, appears, then you also will appear with him in glory" (Col. 3:3–4).
- "Do not be anxious about anything . . ." (Phil. 4:6a). "The Lord is near" (Phil. 4:5b) comes immediately before.
- "Do not wear clothing woven of two kinds of material" (Lev. 19:19c). Notice what precedes all the commands in chapter 19: "The LORD said to Moses, 'Speak to the entire assembly of Israel and say to them: "Be holy because I, the LORD your God, am holy"'" (Lev. 19:1–2).

In short, while we must take the commands of Scripture seriously, we can never reduce the Bible to a series of "naked" exhortations and prohibitions. Those directives come to us clothed in redemptive garb: "This is who your God is! This is what he has done, for his glory and your good! Now live in his love by obeying his commands." We should indeed continue to call our brothers and sisters to live by the commands of God, but let's do it with an awareness of their redemptive context. We will explore that broader relational/redemptive foundation more fully in the next chapter.

The Bible Is *Not* Primarily a Book of Timeless Principles for the Problems of Life

This perspective is related to the first one, but at least this approach to Scripture views the Bible as "bigger" than explicit commands. I would say that this view of the Bible—as the source of principles for living—is the most common view of the Scriptures within evangelicalism. These general ("timeless") principles are then applied to specific contemporary situations.

There are several valid reasons for using the Bible this way. This view of Scripture affirms that you can approach any passage with an application mind-set. You expect to find truth to bring into your present situation, no matter where you are in Scripture, even if the passage does not contain commands. This view also recognizes that some discontinuity exists between the world of the Bible and the readers' world. That is, we can't just move in a direct, 1:1 fashion from the biblical world to our own without at least *some* "translation"—distilling the message of the passage into a principle that can be transported to the present day. This approach also helps with the previous issue of deciding how certain commands are relevant for later times. (Perhaps we should look for the general principle behind the specific admonition for an earlier, specific situation—and then apply that general principle in similar but not identical situations today.) There is some wisdom in this; the consideration of appropriate analogies between then and now does seem warranted.

Further support for this approach comes from the biblical writers themselves, who sometimes appeal to other texts in this principle-oriented, exemplary way. I am currently reading 1 Corinthians and Paul uses the Old Testament Scriptures this way. Here are three examples: (1) He quotes Isaiah 29:14—"I will destroy the wisdom of the wise; the intelligence of the intelligent I will frustrate"—to support his argument that through the cross God has made foolish the wisdom of the world (1:19). (2) Paul uses the story of the Israelites in the wilderness to urge the Corinthians to refrain from setting their hearts "on evil things as they did" (1 Cor. 10:6–11). (3) In 1 Corinthians 5:13 he urges the Corinthians to discipline a man who is involved in sexual immorality with his stepmother: "Expel the wicked man from among you." He appears to be drawing upon multiple passages in Deuteronomy where God instructed the people to deal with immorality among them: "Purge the evil from among you" (Deut. 17:7; 19:19; 21:21; 22:21, 24; 24:7). In almost all those cases, the punishment for the evildoer (who may or may not have been involved in sexual sin) was death by stoning. Paul seems to take the general principle, "You must not tolerate evil within the covenant community," and apply it (without the death penalty) to the Corinthian church.

How might this play out for us? One example from the last chapter falls squarely into this category: the use of Joshua 1 to encourage an evangelistic team as it begins its work. The principle gleaned from Joshua 1:9 might be, "God is present with his people wherever they go, so don't be afraid." It's an added bonus that the biblical and modern contexts are somewhat analogous: in both situations, then and now, God's people are encountering an unbelieving (pagan) culture and require the presence and power of God to succeed. But proponents of this approach to Scripture would say that the situations don't *have* to match to benefit from the principle. For instance, it would be quite easy to use Joshua 1:9 to encourage a person who is terrified about starting a new job. Now, it may well be that one "payoff" of this passage *is* the encouragement to press forward in challenging circumstances. But isn't the use of this verse potentially more meaningful by placing it in the broader context of Joshua, and Scripture at large?

This principle-oriented approach to Scripture overlaps significantly with using the Bible as a topical index of various verses for various problems, although it has a bit more flexibility in its interpretive strategy. Many Bibles have an appendix that highlights the appropriate passages to turn to for certain problems of life. Usually these passages fall into the ditch category—they explicitly mention the problem at hand. So, if you are anxious, turn to Matthew 6:25–34 or 1 Peter 5:7. If you want principles on giving, go to Malachi 3:7–10 or 2 Corinthians 8:1–9.[7] There is, of course, something right about this. A passage that references tithing or giving *ought* to guide our thinking about giving in some way. We *ought* to use passages that discuss worry as we minister to anxious

31

people. The issue is not "Is it appropriate to derive principles for pastoral care from biblical texts?" but rather, "How should we go about doing so?" Is there an approach to the Bible that guides the "how" question?

Viewing the Scriptures first and foremost as the seedbed for general principles creates difficulties. First, there is a continued tendency to overlook the historical, cultural, and social aspects of the Bible. In the previous chapter I talked about the necessity of considering these contextual elements of a passage. Strictly speaking, there are no "timeless texts" of Scripture. *All* Scripture arises in a particular historical context for particular pastoral purposes. "The texts of Scripture both presuppose and are ordered to communities of faith, in all their concreteness, richness, and messiness."[8] Overlooking these concrete occasions for God's revelation may lead to unwise conclusions about what principles a particular passage might generate. In fact, rather than *draw out* principles from texts, it is all too easy to *read* principles *into* a text to support a cherished belief, especially when a text is detached from its particular place in God's redemptive history.

Second, similar to what we saw with the rule-oriented approach, this view of the Bible leans toward the triumph of the principle over the person. In the Bible God speaks to his people. Scripture is passion-filled, truthful communication that reveals the character and work of God, tailored to the pressing needs of God's people. Such discourse resists being reduced to principles and propositions, although it is not opposed to such activity (as we saw when Paul used portions of the Old Testament in a principle-oriented way).[9]

Again, I am urging a fuller, richer way to approach and apply Scripture that is most in line with its redemptive-historical character. There's buried treasure to be found that will make your use of commands and principles wiser and more nuanced!

The Bible Is *Not* Primarily a Casebook of Characters to Imitate or Avoid

This is a variation of the preceding view of the Bible. This approach highlights particular characters in Scripture (and there are a lot of them!) and asks, "What should I think, say, or do based on the ways these characters were portrayed? What example do they give me to follow or avoid?"

Again, there is scriptural warrant for this in the way New Testament writers appeal to the Old Testament. Consider James 5:10–11: "Brothers, as an example of patience in the face of suffering, take the prophets who spoke in the name of the Lord. As you know, we consider blessed those who have persevered. You have heard of Job's perseverance and have seen what the Lord finally brought about. The Lord is full of compassion and mercy." Later in the same chapter James points to Elijah to illustrate his point that the "prayer of a righteous man is powerful and effective" (5:16b). He notes, "Elijah was a man just like us. He prayed earnestly that it would not rain, and it did not rain on the land for three and a half years. Again he prayed, and the heavens gave rain, and the earth produced its crops" (5:17–18). I don't know about you, but I'm stunned to consider Elijah and myself on the same playing field. But that is the connection James is making!

In John's first epistle, as a follow-up to his command, "We should love one another" (3:11), John exhorts, "Do not be like Cain, who belonged to the evil one and murdered his brother" (3:12a). John is saying in effect, "Do you want an example of anti-love? Look at Cain, who murdered his brother! You can't call yourself a Christian and hate your brother. Don't do what Cain did!"

I've already mentioned Paul's instruction to the Corinthians, laced with references to the wilderness community: "Now these things occurred as examples to keep us from setting our hearts on evil things as they did" (1 Cor. 10:6). Specifically Paul exhorts, "Do not be idolaters, as some of them were" (10:7). "We should not commit sexual immorality, as some of them did" (10:8). "We should not test the Lord, as some of them did" (10:9). "And do not grumble, as some of them did" (10:10). Paul applies the example of the Israelites further by warning the Corinthians, "So, if you think you are standing firm, be careful that you don't fall!" (10:12). Basically he says in this series of verses, "Don't do what they did. Instead, be careful, lest you fall also."

The New Testament writers also appeal to the example of Jesus himself. The writer of Hebrews says, "Consider him

[Jesus] who endured such opposition from sinful men, so that you will not grow weary and lose heart" (Heb. 12:3). Peter speaks to a persecuted community, "But if you suffer for doing good and you endure it, this is commendable before God. To this you were called, because Christ suffered for you, leaving you an example, that you should follow in his steps. 'He committed no sin, and no deceit was found in his mouth.' When they hurled their insults at him, he did not retaliate; when he suffered, he made no threats. Instead, he entrusted himself to him who judges justly" (1 Pet. 2:20b–23). Finally, John says, "This is how we know what love is: Jesus Christ laid down his life for us. And we ought to lay down our lives for our brothers" (1 John 3:16). In each case the writers appeal to Jesus as an exemplar for faith and obedience. What is highlighted is not so much the redemptive work of Christ but his character in action.

In a similar way, we might read about David, the man after God's own heart, in 1 Samuel, contrasting his character and actions with those of Saul. In those chapters David displays unwavering trust in God, courage, humility, patience, and wisdom.[10] Someone using Scripture this way might also find positive examples in Joseph's sexual purity (Gen. 39), Moses' intercession (Exod. 32), Josiah's spiritual zeal (2 Kings 22—23), Daniel's devotion (Dan. 1), and Stephen's courage (Acts 7), to name a few. Negative examples might include Abraham's fear (Gen. 12:10–20), Aaron's idolatry and poor leadership (Exod. 32), Solomon's lusts (1 Kings 11), and the deceit of Ananias and Sapphira (Acts 5).

I recently heard a version of this approach to Scripture at a seminary graduation. The speaker's text was the feeding of the five thousand (John 6:1–13). He drew his hearers into the story from the perspective of the small boy who supplied the loaves and fish for the miracle. The take-home message was, "OK, seminary graduates, you now have in your possession five loaves and two fish. It isn't much, but will you take your stuff (talents, education, gifts, passions, etc.) to the Master to see what he'll do with it?" In other words, they were to have the faith to do what the boy did! For this speaker, even a "minor" character served as an example.

What's helpful about this approach? First, if you're in ministry, it's natural to empathize with the people God has placed in your life. Their stories ought to draw you in so that you "rejoice with those who rejoice; [and] mourn with those who mourn" (Rom. 12:15). You try to understand their point of view, their struggles, their triumphs, the highs and lows of their faith. It's hard to stay detached—and that's a good thing! Why should this be any different when we encounter people in Scripture? Why shouldn't we feel the thrill of their victory or the agony of their defeat? Why shouldn't we emulate the pattern of their faith or avoid the example of their unbelief?

Second, a character- or example-oriented approach can highlight that God reveals himself to people who have the same basic problems we do. To borrow a phrase from the hymn "Jesus! What a Friend for Sinners!" the people of God in the Old Testament and New Testament are "tempted, tried, and sometimes failing."[11] They needed a Savior also! They needed the resources of the Redeemer to live in a fallen world, just as we do. They needed wisdom from God in order to live rightly. Identifying with the characters in Scripture helps us recognize the specific ways God acts and speaks, mercifully and justly, to his suffering and sinful people. In the pages of Scripture, God initiates relationship with real people, not cardboard cutouts! It helps struggling people to see struggling people in the pages of Scripture. This reminds us that the God who draws near to the struggler "is the same yesterday and today and forever" (Heb. 13:8).

But here is a shortcoming of this approach: it doesn't *necessarily* help us understand the overall plot that incorporates all of these characters, praiseworthy or not. In contrast to the last paragraph, it doesn't *necessarily* highlight the character and work of God. As we will see in the next chapter, the Bible is a story of God that goes somewhere. The characters within its pages play a supporting role to the God who engineers history and then authors the telling of it. The endpoint is not to imitate David, Hannah, or Paul per se, but to relate intimately to the God of David, Hannah, and Paul, who orchestrates history to accomplish his redemptive purposes. The characters are signposts to the pursuing, redeeming love of God.

To return to an earlier example, while it may be appropriate to draw some application from the boy in the feeding of the five thousand, what we *can't* miss is Jesus! He is the One who sustains his people, who satisfies their spiritual hunger. Ultimately, he is the bread from heaven, broken for his people. He is the Father's manna in the flesh (John 6:32–35). Why shouldn't I want to bring my gifts and training to lay at the feet of such a gracious One? Do you notice something here? I essentially ended up with the same application as the seminary graduation speaker but with a Christ-oriented emphasis. The boy in the story may serve as a touchstone for application, but his example doesn't carry the full "freight" of this passage.

To conclude, there may indeed be a place for using characters as examples to follow or avoid—remember, the biblical writers do it too—so long as it is practiced with an awareness of the Christ-centered plotline of the Bible.

The Bible Is *Not* Primarily a System of Doctrines

No doubt, the study of the Bible can and should lead to theological reflection. This has been going on since the earliest days of the church. It is helpful for the church to consider how to organize the Bible's teaching. In fact, the work of arranging the teachings of Scripture into comprehensive and coherent doctrinal formulations has often (usually!) been done to resolve pressing problems or controversies in the church.[12] These doctrinal conclusions then serve as guardrails for further Scripture study and theological reflection. This organization of biblical teaching over the centuries[13] reminds us that the Spirit's illuminating work hasn't begun with our generation. We stand on the shoulders of those who have studied and arranged the teachings of Scripture topically, whether we are aware of it or not.

But what are some problems with functionally viewing Scripture *primarily* as a series of doctrinal formulations? First, it can minimize the depth and breadth of biblical wisdom. Systematic theology helps to distill the Bible's teachings, but it does not exhaust the complexity of what God means to say to the church. In a similar way, a book report may accurately outline and summarize a book's contents, but it is no substitute for reading the book cover to cover, pondering, relishing, and wrestling through its details. We never want to make an outline, however comprehensive and accurate, a substitute for God's multifaceted personal communication through his Word.

A second problem is the if-you're-a-hammer-everything's-a-nail syndrome. You will have a tendency to approach texts expecting (and perhaps seeking) to support certain theological beliefs—the Trinity, the nature of the atonement, predestination, free will, justification by faith, rapture of the saints, hell, and many others.[14] This may or may not be appropriate based on the text(s) under consideration. The problem in this approach is that the Bible can be reduced to a set of proof-texts that support key doctrines.[15]

Viewing the Bible in systematic categories may lead to over-emphasizing certain passages or books and deemphasizing others based on your theological predispositions. What is the result? The Bible's wonderfully varied terrain becomes "flattened." Michael Williams notes, "The complexity and ambiguity of reality is lost in the press toward univocal neatness and rational fit, and the dynamics of events and relationships is reduced to broad generalities."[16]

A Gospel-Deficient Bible?!

I have saved for last the most serious deficiency of these approaches to the Bible. Certainly, all four of them extract biblical texts from the flow of history. But if you minimize the historical outworking of God, you potentially minimize the centrality of the death, resurrection, ascension, and return of Jesus Christ! That's where history is going! (See 1 Cor. 15:20–28.) Notice that you could talk about how to discipline your child with the rod (a rule, based on Prov. 23:13–14), draw encouragement from God's presence as you start a demanding new job (a general principle, from Isa. 41:10), emulate David's courage (a character example, from 1 Sam. 17), and discuss predestination (a doctrine from Eph. 1), without ever referring to the coming of the kingdom in Jesus Christ *or* encountering him yourself! Shouldn't the life, death, and resurrection of Christ have some practical connection to disciplining children, God's presence, living with courage, and the doctrine of predestination? Of course it should—and it does. As we will see, the whole framework of the New Testament is that Jesus the King has come. That's the gospel (Mark 1:15)! That's good news for sufferers and sinners!

This redemptive-historical approach to Scripture in no way minimizes the importance of commands, principles, characters, and doctrine in Scripture. Rather, it puts all of them in a gospel-centered, relational framework. It highlights that the Bible is God's "show-and-tell": his mighty acts of redemption on behalf of sinners, told for the purpose of restoring broken relationship with his image bearers. As I mentioned in the last chapter, this should enrich and deepen your approach to Scripture and to people. Don't be discouraged if your current view or use of Scripture frequently falls into one or more of the categories I mentioned in this chapter. Consider the example of Apollos (Acts 18:24–26) as an encouragement:

> Meanwhile a Jew named Apollos, a native of Alexandria, came to Ephesus. He was a learned man, with a thorough knowledge of the Scriptures. He had been instructed in the way of the Lord, and he spoke with great fervor and taught about Jesus accurately, though he knew only the baptism of John. He began to speak boldly in the synagogue. When Priscilla and Aquila heard him, they invited him to their home and explained to him the way of God more adequately.

What do I want you to see here? God clearly used Apollos to preach the gospel *before* he met Priscilla and Aquila and gained a fuller understanding of the gospel (which included, presumably, the baptism of the Holy Spirit). He wasn't doing anything wrong or unwise, and he taught accurately. But he had room to grow in his understanding of God's redemptive plan. So do all of us! This book is the fruit of my own growth in understanding. I hope you will conclude that within these pages is a "more adequate" approach to Scripture and to people, which will only further and deepen your already active ministry.

In the next chapter we'll explore what the Bible *is,* and see how it sets the stage for wise application of Scripture to life.

Discussion Questions

1. Consider the ways you heard, read, and/or ministered the Scriptures this past week. Which view(s) of the Bible mentioned above are most characteristic of your life, your community, and your ministry?
2. Where have you seen these view(s) of the Bible helpful in your life and ministry? Where have you seen them to be problematic or deficient?
3. Do you think each passage of Scripture should lead to a principle for living or to some doctrinal proposition? Why or why not?

CHAPTER 3

What the Bible Is

In the last chapter I surveyed views of the Bible that do not do full justice to its essential character as the progressive, personal revelation of God to his people. This chapter argues for the essential "story form" or "narrative structure" of the Bible as the means God uses to make himself known. If you read the Bible from cover to cover you realize that it narrates (proclaims!) a true and cohesive story: the good news that through Jesus Christ God has entered history to liberate and renew the world from its bondage to sin and suffering. This is the story of God, who pursues the restoration of his creation at the cost of his own life. He is making all things new (Rev. 21:5)! That's the simple and yet profound, life- and world-altering plotline of the Bible. Don't you want to live in light of that plot? Don't you want to help others do the same? No part of our lives should remain unchanged as we are captured by this redemptive story.

I Love to Tell the *Story*

Do you feel a bit uncomfortable using the "s" word when it comes to the Bible? Perhaps it relates to the way our culture views stories. When we think of "story" we think "fairy tale," "made up," or "fiction."

And yet much of our lives are spent telling and listening to "stories." People tell stories all the time. Think about when you meet someone for the first time. How do you get to know him? Unless you are interviewing him for a job, you don't begin by asking for a résumé of the bare facts of his life! You ask questions and listen. And the shape of his story—how he interprets and presents the details of his life to you—prompts further questions from you. And so the dialogue develops. But you're not thinking (hopefully!), *You're making this up*. Or *That may be your take on your life, but let me do some objective research from other sources.*

What happens when you get home at the end of the day and your son asks, "Mom, what did you do today?" You don't pull out your Day-Timer and say, "Here, look at my appointment schedule." No, you narrate (tell the story of) your day. You don't share every detail ("First, I turned off the alarm clock. No, I guess I hit the snooze button initially. Then I stumbled out of the bed to the bathroom. . . ."). OK, too much information! You pick and choose the most meaningful aspects of your day and tell a short story. It's a true story, but it's not an exhaustive, videotaped account of your day. You might think of this kind of storytelling as "interpreted personal history," which could be autobiographical (told by yourself) or biographical (told by someone else). Notice that the goal of this storytelling is not merely to share information but to build relationship.

In a similar way, the Bible tells a true tale from God's perspective through the individual voices of the human authors. The Bible is God's story, his declaration of the way the world really is. The Bible is not an exhaustive history of the world, but it narrates, in a progressive way over time, the story of God's actions and what they mean for the people of God. As with the working mother and her inquiring child, this is no bare recounting of facts. This is no mere documentary. Rather, God reveals himself to restore relationship with his people. He enters history to rescue his creation and then proclaims that fact through the many writers of Scripture. This means that every part of God's story has personal impact, to help us and others grow in our faith. I believe that impact is even greater when we understand how the various parts of the Bible contribute to the overall redemptive plotline.

The Chapters of the Story

Can the plotline of the Bible be described more specifically? In other words, what are the different elements that compose the larger drama?

Ben Witherington summarizes it like this: "It is a Story that focuses on God's relationship to humankind, from the beginning of the human race in Adam to its climax in the eschatological [i.e., last] Adam, and beyond. It is a Story about creation and creature and their redemption by, in, and through Jesus Christ. It is a Story about a community of faith created out of the midst of fallen humanity."[1]

In addition, there is a long history, particularly in the Dutch Calvinist tradition, of seeing the Bible as telling the story of Creation, Fall, and Redemption (or perhaps, New Creation).[2] Genesis 1—2 tells the story of the creation of the world culminating in the creation of humans as image bearers of God. It also reveals God's design for his image bearers in Genesis 1:28. Genesis 3 tells of Adam and Eve's fall into sin with disastrous consequences for themselves and all of creation. But Genesis also gives hints of future redemption in God's cursing of the serpent (3:14–16) and in God's preservation of Adam and Eve. God's redemption begins in earnest with the calling of Abram (Abraham) in Genesis 12, through whom all nations would be blessed. Redemption, of course, reaches its climax in the coming of Jesus Christ, who in his person and work ushers in the new creation (2 Cor. 5:17).

Craig Bartholomew and Michael Goheen helpfully structure the biblical narrative as a six-act play:[3]

- Act 1. God establishes his kingdom: Creation
- Act 2. Rebellion in the kingdom: Fall
- Act 3. The King chooses Israel: Redemption initiated
- Act 4. The coming of the King: Redemption accomplished
- Act 5. Spreading the news of the King: The mission of the church
- Act 6. The return of the King: Redemption completed

There are several advantages to this summary. First, it highlights the importance of the kingdom of God as an overarching theme of the Bible, succinctly described elsewhere as "God's people in God's place under God's rule."[4] Second, it reminds us that God initiated redemption for his people in the Old Testament, the "prototype" being the exodus, thus highlighting the importance of Israel for understanding what happens in the New Testament. But third, it reminds us that the coming of King Jesus is the culmination of the longed-for redemption anticipated in the Old Testament, so that the story of Israel and the story of Jesus Christ are intimately connected. Fourth, this outline highlights the importance of the church for God's ongoing redemptive work in the world, showing, at least in a general way, where we fit into the story. Act 5 might well be called "The King and We" (with apologies to Rodgers and Hammerstein!) because God's continuing mission in the world is tied to his presence with the church, the body of Christ, through the indwelling of the Holy Spirit.

More personally, this kingdom-centered plotline of Scripture reveals our true identity and gives us real purpose for living. As believers we find our identity as brothers and sisters of the King. We are royal siblings of our elder brother Jesus (Heb. 2:5–18), who brings to fruition the Father's supreme rule on earth. We are coheirs with Christ (Rom. 8:15–17; 1 Pet. 1:3–5). This identity is wedded to a mission: to proclaim the reign of our King and to help restore lives in keeping with his love and truth-filled rule. In the day-to-day ordinariness of our lives, and perhaps particularly in the face of struggle, it is difficult to grasp that we are part of a larger story in which we play a vital part. A kingdom-centered or Christ-centered view of Scripture keeps our royal identity and purpose always before us.

Jesus Christ, the Pivot Point of the Story[5]

It is clear from the outlines noted above that the coming of the kingdom in Jesus Christ is the climax of the biblical story. But where in Scripture do we see this? We see this in the way the New Testament presents the life and ministry of Jesus as the fulfillment of Israel's story. Moreover, we hear it in the way that Jesus speaks of his life in connection with the Old Testament Scriptures. Finally, we see it in the way the New Testament writers use the Old Testament, in effect retelling and advancing the story of Israel and God's kingdom in light of Jesus the Messiah.

Jesus, the True Israelite

First, note how the general characteristics of Jesus' life connect with Israel. In fact, you might say that he is *the* representative Israelite.[6] His human ancestry is traced backward to David and Abraham (Matt. 1:1) and ultimately to Adam, "the son of God" (Luke 3:38). He sojourns in Egypt (Matt. 2:13–15). He undergoes baptism through water and is declared to be God's Son, like the Israelites who were "baptized" in the Red Sea crossing (Hos. 11:1; Matt. 3:15, 17; 1 Cor. 10:2). Like Israel, he undergoes temptation in the wilderness but, unlike Israel, he prevails (Matt. 4:1–11). He declares and explains the Law to the people as did Moses from Mount Sinai (Matt. 5—7). He keeps the Law perfectly (John 8:46; 2 Cor. 5:21; Heb. 4:15; 1 Pet. 2:22; 1 John 3:5). He is the embodiment of God's kingdom (Luke 17:21; John 18:36).

But he completes Israel's story in an unexpected way. He does not reestablish the renewing rule of God by freeing the Jews from exile and from enemy rule in accordance with Old Testament prophetic declarations (e.g., Isa. 52:7–10; 59:16–20; Zech. 8:3). Instead, he becomes the Passover Lamb, the final sacrifice for the sins of his people (Matt. 20:28; 1 Cor. 5:7; Heb. 9:11–15; 10:11–14). Suffering, humiliation, a cross, and death would precede glory. Sacrifice would precede celebration and vindication.

In Tolkien's *The Return of the King,* Aragorn was the one upon whom the hopes of Middle Earth largely depended. Imagine if he had died in humiliation on the battlefield rather than prevailing as victor and then rightfully ascending his throne! "Wait a minute," people might have said, "we thought he was the one who would redeem Gondor. But he lies dead and with him our hopes have died." Doesn't that sound like the discouragement of the disciples on the road to Emmaus (Luke 24:21)?

The (first) coming of King Jesus was in humility and self-sacrifice (Phil. 2:5–11). But his death was not the end of the story. His resurrection from the dead proved his identity as the Messiah, the King, the Son of God (Rom. 1:3–4). He was not a failed, humiliated Messiah "wannabe." The resurrection shows that Jesus was no pretender to the throne. He was (is) God's anointed Son, for whom death could not have the final say. With Jesus' death and resurrection, the new age of the Spirit dawned. The future broke into the present. As N. T. Wright notes, what the Jews expected at the end of history (e.g., resurrection of the dead, vindication of God's people over their enemies, the age to come manifested by the everlasting reign of God among his people) God accomplished in and for Jesus Christ in the middle of history.[7]

Why is this important to keep in mind as we minister to others? First, if Jesus is the fulfillment of Israel's story, we who are in Christ are intimately connected with God's people in the Old Testament. Adam and Eve, Abraham, Moses, David, Jeremiah, Esther—they are all part of our family tree! This should highlight the relevance of the Old Testament for us who have been engrafted, through Christ, into Israel's destiny (Rom. 9—11). All the covenantal blessings of Israel come to us through Jesus.

Secondly, the way Jesus completes Israel's story suggests an overall pattern for our own Christian lives. What are your expectations for what the reign of Jesus looks like in your life and in your friends' lives? Consider Paul's words: "I want to know Christ and the power of his resurrection and the fellowship of sharing in his sufferings, becoming like him in his death, and so, somehow, to attain to the resurrection from the dead" (Phil. 3:10–11). You might wish that Paul had stopped after "I want to know Christ and the power of his resurrection"! Me too! Triumph over evil, victory over sin, glory. But Paul includes "sharing in his sufferings" and "becoming like him in his death" on the journey to experiencing resurrection. That is the way of the King. That is how he has chosen to bring his renewing rule. Suffering precedes glory. Death precedes resurrection. Grace to his people comes at the cost of his life. This way of the cross remains the pattern for our lives until Jesus returns to bring an end to sin and suffering (cf. Luke 9:22–24; 1 Cor. 2:1–5; Gal. 2:20; Phil. 2:5–8; Heb. 12:2–3; 1 Pet. 2:20b–25). We follow in our Savior's self-sacrificial footsteps.[8] This view of Christ helps us to persevere in the hardships of ministry. It provides a realistic vision for the Christian life that we set before ourselves and others, especially when we are tempted to think that life in Christ is about our personal fulfillment and happiness.

"It's All About Me"

Second, Jesus saw his ministry as the fulfillment of the (Old Testament) Scriptures. Notice how Jesus inaugurates his ministry in Luke 4. Jesus quotes Isaiah 61:1–2, which speaks of Israel's return from exile and then states, "Today this scripture is fulfilled in your hearing" (Luke 4:21). Jesus is in essence saying, "Your long exile is over. Release from your oppression and the brokenness of all creation is at hand through me." Referring more comprehensively to the Old Testament Scriptures, Jesus says in Matthew 5:17, "Do not think that I have come to abolish the Law or the Prophets; I have not come to abolish them but to fulfill them." In other words, the trajectory of the arrow shot from the Hebrew Scriptures finds its target (fulfillment) in Jesus of Nazareth.

Perhaps one of the best examples of this view of the Old Testament coming to fruition in Jesus is seen in Luke 24.[9] Here Jesus comes upon two disciples on the road to Emmaus and talks with them about the events of the last few days. The disciples, who are kept from recognizing him, lament the crucifixion and death of Jesus, upon whom their messianic (kingdom) hopes were placed. They also express bewilderment about the secondhand report that he was alive. Jesus responded, "How foolish you are, and how slow of heart to believe all that the prophets have spoken! Did not the Christ [Messiah] have to suffer these things and then enter his glory?" (vv. 25–26). Luke goes on to write, "And beginning with Moses and all the Prophets, he explained to them what was said in all the Scriptures concerning himself" (v. 27).

Later Jesus tells a gathered group of disciples, "Everything must be fulfilled that is written about me in the Law of Moses, the Prophets and the Psalms" (v. 44). Note that Jesus is referring to the Hebrew Scriptures comprehensively: (1) the Law of Moses (i.e., Torah—Genesis through Deuteronomy); (2) the Prophets, which includes the historical books (Joshua through Kings) in addition to Isaiah, Jeremiah, Ezekiel, and the Twelve ("Minor" prophets); and (3) the Psalms, which are representative of the

"Writings," the third division of the Hebrew Scriptures. In other words, the entirety of the Hebrew Scriptures (our Old Testament) testifies to the coming Messiah, Jesus.

Even more amazing, Jesus goes on to summarize what is written in the Old Testament: "The Christ will suffer and rise from the dead on the third day, and repentance and forgiveness of sins will be preached in his name to all nations, beginning at Jerusalem" (vv. 46–47). Really?! Is that in the Old Testament? Explicitly, no. In essence, yes. As Dan McCartney says, "There is no single Old Testament passage where these elements all occur. Rather, it appears that Jesus is giving the disciples the key to understanding the Old Testament as a whole."[10]

Basically, Jesus is saying, "I am the lens through which you must look at the Old Testament. I am the interpretive key that opens its treasure chest of meaning. If you miss how the Old Testament testifies about me, you will miss where the story of redemption is going." This Christ-shaped (gospel-shaped) lens profoundly affects the way we go about interpreting and applying Scripture. This lens keeps our approach to Scripture "familial" and relational because we yearn to see Jesus in its pages. We desire to learn of the One in whom "we live and move and have our being" (Acts 17:28). And, as I mentioned earlier, it keeps as our purpose the mission of our King, to heal the brokenness of people and the world around us.

(Re)Telling the Old, Old Story

Third, New Testament writers anchor their message in the life, death, and resurrection of Jesus Christ as the fulfillment of Israel's story. Take a look at Luke's account of Paul preaching in Pisidian Antioch (Acts 13:13–41).[11] Consider this the biblical equivalent of a ZIP drive or perhaps the "Cliff Notes" version of redemptive history! Paul begins his sermon with God's choosing of the Patriarchs, then hits the high points of Jewish history: the exodus, wilderness wanderings, possession of the Promised Land, the era of the judges, and finally the Davidic monarchy, from whom Jesus the Savior descended (v. 23). Following this summary Paul proclaims the good news to the Jews and God-fearing Gentiles who were present: "What God promised our fathers he has fulfilled for us, their children, by raising up Jesus. . . .Therefore, my brothers, I want you to know that through Jesus the forgiveness of sins is proclaimed to you. Through him everyone who believes is justified from everything you could not be justified from by the law of Moses" (vv. 32, 38–39). Paul sees the universal scope of the Messiah's work as he commits to the ingathering of the Gentiles (vv. 46–48), which was to be part of Israel's destiny (Gen. 12:3; Isa. 49:6).

Paul connects the Old Testament Scriptures with the coming of Jesus in two ways: promise/fulfillment and problem/solution. All that God had promised in the Old Testament was fulfilled in the ministry of Jesus Christ, whose presence heralded the new beginning, the restoration from sin and suffering that Old Testament writers had longed for.[12] What God had promised resounded as a "Yes!" in Christ Jesus (2 Cor. 1:20). But Jesus is also a solution to the seemingly never-ending drift of God's people into disobedience and apostasy, a problem that riddles much of the Old Testament. Who can cure the backsliding of God's people? How can creation be rescued from brokenness and decay? Jesus does what Israel could not do. He brings restoration that the Law could not accomplish (Rom. 8:3). Jesus gives us new hearts and places his Spirit within his people (cf. Ezek. 36:26–27). He is the author of a new and everlasting covenant, one that cannot be broken (cf. Jer. 31:31–34). Preconversion, life for Paul was Torah (law)-shaped. After conversion, it was cross-shaped (or perhaps, just as appropriately, Spirit-shaped).

Throughout his writings, "Paul refers to four interrelated stories comprising one larger drama: (1) the story of a world gone wrong; (2) the story of Israel in that world; (3) the story of Christ, which arises out of the story of Israel and humankind on the human side of things, but in a larger sense arises out of the very story of God as creator and redeemer; and (4) the story of Christians, including Paul himself, which arises out of all three of these previous stories and is the first full installment of the story of a world set right again."[13]

In summary, the Old Testament should be seen as preparation for and anticipation of the King's coming. The New Testament should be seen as the proclamation that God's expected reign has come in Jesus, with the cosmic and ethical implications of this fact worked out in many new contexts. The New Testament's thrust is: now that God has established his kingdom, what are the implications of this gospel (good news)? That's why each book of the New Testament doesn't simply rehearse or rehash the barest essentials of the story—Christ died, Christ was raised, Christ will come again (cf. 1 Cor. 15:3). No, rather than playing the exact same melody again and again, the New Testament writers transpose it and arrange it for new contexts and audiences. But the narrative anchor point is always Jesus and his kingdom, and the subsequent pouring out of the Spirit upon the church at Pentecost.

Thus, the Scriptures find their unity in Jesus. Through him, God the Creator and Redeemer accomplishes his salvation. Through Jesus, God the Spirit is poured out upon and indwells his people (Acts 2:32–33). Old Testament books find their ultimate meaning and fulfillment in him. New Testament books anchor their reflections on the coming of the kingdom in Jesus and anticipate the day he will return to consummate his kingdom. The life, death, and resurrection of Jesus is both the endpoint and starting point for the biblical writers. As Chris Wright says, "Jesus, then, is not only (looking back) the end of the beginning [i.e., the completion of the story that began in Genesis]; he is also (looking forward) the beginning of the end [i.e., the firstfruits of a new creation]."[14] He is the pivot point of the story! As Ben Witherington affirms, "Christ's story is the hinge, crucial turning point, and climax of the entire larger drama, which more than anything else affects how *the* Story will ultimately turn out. The Story contracts to Christ, the seed of Abraham, and then once again expands to include Christ's many followers."[15]

We should view the New Testament as the Spirit-inspired proclamation *and* application of Christ's death and resurrection to the lives of God's people. It proclaims him as the fulfillment of Old Testament promises, the solution to the problem of sin and suffering. It applies that reality by demonstrating how the character of Christ is increasingly formed in believers' lives in many different situations. A Christ-centered lens makes sense of the Bible as a whole and it reveals the One who is the focus of our lives. If we want to grow in love for God and for neighbor, we can't miss Christ, the hope of glory (Col. 1:27).

Words with a Punch

It's important to realize that the Bible not only tells a true story; it also demands a response. The authors of Scripture write with intention—their words are meant to provoke a response from the reader. In other words, the Bible is a story that provokes action! It not only informs; it also transforms our lives. It's a message that invites us to turn from unbelief and to participate in the life of the One who, through his death and resurrection, forgives our sins and gives us new life through the Spirit.

Consider Peter's sermon at Pentecost: "When the people heard this [Jesus as Lord and Messiah], they were cut to the heart and said to Peter and the other apostles, 'Brothers, what shall we do?' Peter replied, 'Repent and be baptized, every one of you, in the name of Jesus Christ for the forgiveness of your sins. And you will receive the gift of the Holy Spirit'" (Acts 2:37–38). At another time Peter reminded his hearers that God raised up Jesus so that they might turn from their wicked ways (Acts 3:26). Jesus called Paul "to open their [the Gentiles'] eyes and turn them from darkness to light, and from the power of Satan to God, so that they may receive forgiveness of sins and a place among those who are sanctified by faith in me" (Acts 26:18).

This impulse toward transformation into the character of Christ (sanctification) is particularly seen in Paul's letters, many of which have what is called an "indicative-imperative" structure. It goes like this: Given what God has done in Jesus Christ (*indicative*), this is how you should live (*imperative*).[16] So, for example, Ephesians 1—3 focuses primarily on the "what" of the triune God's salvation and Ephesians 4—6 focuses on the "so what," the implications of this salvation for the church at Ephesus.

But notice, *all* of Scripture is written with a pastoral intent, not simply the "imperative" portions. The books of the Bible are meant to provoke a response in God's people, whether it be worship, conviction of sin, joy, deeds of justice and mercy, praise, prayer, concern for the lost, and so forth. All Scripture invites a response to God. In this sense, all Scripture is "practical theology"—narrative with a punch! As David Powlison notes, "Because Scripture reveals God at work, the Scriptures *are* practical theology. We read truth in action. We witness relevant truth. We hear an applied revelation."[17]

But for us it's more than holy eavesdropping. We are not merely listening to a conversation God had with his people several thousand years ago, trying to extract some benefit for our own lives. We are part of the same story line. We are included in God's great rescue operation. Israel's Messiah is our Messiah. The apostles' Lord and Savior is our Lord and Savior. That's why it's so critical to see the Bible as God's unfolding story of salvation that centers on Jesus Christ. As part of the new family the Father is creating in Christ Jesus, we own the Scriptures as our family history. If we miss Jesus as the fulfillment of Old Testament messianic expectations and the foundation of New Testament kingdom proclamation, we unwittingly distance ourselves from the contemporary relevance of the Bible. He, through the Spirit, is the living link between the story of Scripture and the stories of our lives.

By the mercy of God, this story, this Word, became ours when we were united by faith to our crucified and risen Savior. It's *his* story and it's *our* story by virtue of being his! So, then, the Bible is a book primed for application.[18] While Scripture passages may not be "timeless texts," they are certainly "timely texts" for the people of God.[19]

In the next chapter we'll explore the practical implications of viewing the Bible as Christ-centered redemptive history.

Discussion Questions

1. Are you persuaded that the Bible is one cohesive story centered on the coming of the kingdom in Jesus? Why or why not? Are there other ways to understand the Bible as a whole?

2. How might seeing the Bible in this way both simplify and complicate your use of Scripture in ministry?

3. Starting with some of the ideas in this chapter, what implications does a redemptive-historical or Christ-centered view of Scripture have for the way we interpret and use the Bible in ministry? (This prepares you for the focus of the next chapter.)

CHAPTER 4

Implications
for Reading and Using
the Bible

If the Bible is one story with Jesus and his kingdom as the focal point, how should this impact the way we interpret and use Scripture in ministry? Here are some initial suggestions. We will expand these ideas in later chapters.

1. We Read Back to Front and Front to Back

To interpret and apply the Bible wisely, we should develop the habit of reading Scripture "back to front" and "front to back."[1] What does it mean to read the Bible back to front? It means rereading any text (particularly Old Testament passages) in light of the end of the story—the coming of the kingdom in Jesus Christ. I wrote the original draft for this chapter on the eve of the much-anticipated release of the final book of the Harry Potter series. I knew that when I finished that book, *Harry Potter and the Deathly Hallows,* the ending would forever change the way I read and understood the details of the earlier books. Sure enough, details that *seemed* so significant were no longer so once I knew the entire story. Details that had been easy to overlook now grew in their significance in light of the story's end.² "So *that's* what it meant!" "So *that's* what was really going on in that scene."

We can have this back-to-front experience watching movies as well. Have you watched *A Beautiful Mind,* the story of mathematician and schizophrenic John Nash? I remember thinking early on in the movie, *If I were John Nash, I would be paranoid, too, given all the stress and secrecy of his government intelligence job!* Of course, we later come to learn that his hiring by the government, the code-breaking work he was doing, and even some of his friends (e.g., his college roommate) were fabrications of his mind. What seemed so real, even to the viewer, were actually hallucinations. The end of the story forced me to see earlier parts in a new light.³

Similarly, knowing the end of the biblical story means we can never read the earlier parts in the same way. That's certainly true for the way Jesus and the New Testament writers read and interpreted the (Old Testament) Scriptures, as we saw in the last chapter. Knowing how the story ends, we ask, "What difference does the death and resurrection of Jesus make for how I understand this passage?"⁴ The death and resurrection of Jesus Christ is the climax of redemption initiated in the Old Testament and the sure foundation for the life of the newly formed church. The New Testament writers consider what the reality of the new creation (ushered in by Christ's death and resurrection) should look like in the life of the church, even as they anticipate the ultimate end of the story, the return of Christ. So, whether we find ourselves in the Old Testament or New Testament, we expect to discover an organic connection to the person and work of Christ, with multifaceted implications for the lives of God's people.

It's also true that we must read the Bible front to back. This means we take seriously where a particular text falls in the historical outworking of the story for at least three reasons. The first reason has to do with the idea of the Bible as "practical theology," introduced in the previous chapter. The Bible is, in fact, an evolving practical theology by God's design. God reveals himself personally to his people in specific contexts over time. God shapes his Word to the evolving needs of his people. This prompts us to ask, "What does God reveal about himself in this book or passage that helps the recipients of his message?" How wonderful to realize that God does not reveal himself "generically" but in multifaceted and specific ways! Sitting with the details and historical context of a passage primes us for application as we observe God's Word matched to specific human need. Further, it encourages me to ask how I might step into a particular story and see how God's particularized grace connects to *my* situation.

Second, in a related way, reading front to back guards us from oversimplifying the plotline of Scripture. The coming of the kingdom in Jesus as the climax of the story doesn't mean that you "shoehorn" him artificially into every text. In our zeal to acknowledge the redemptive-historical character of Scripture, we don't want to insist that every passage is about Jesus *explicitly*. Rather the themes of each book, tailored to its historical context, contribute *implicitly* to our understanding of the kingdom. Each passage or book adds its distinctive voice to a swelling chorus that says, "New creation has come through King Jesus!" (I'll discuss in later chapters how to capitalize on the distinctives of a passage while keeping it tied to the broader redemptive plotline of Scripture.)

Third, details matter. Think about an accident scene investigation. The end of the story is clear; the debris lies on the road to prove it. But the details of the story matter. One driver fumbling for his cell phone. Another driver checking on her kids in the rearview mirror. The overlooked turn signal. Exceeding the speed limit. All these details contribute to the total understanding of the story. These details *lead* somewhere and are important in and of themselves.

In reality, the ending of a story only makes sense in light of what has come before. The more captivated we are by the details, the more glorious will seem the story's climax. The more puzzled we are by the details, the more clarity (and perhaps surprise!) comes with the climax. The more we understand the significance of the details, the more significant the climax. If Jesus is the fulfillment of Israel's story in his first and second comings, we need to pay attention to the ways the redemptive story builds up to Christ and then flows out from him through the Spirit. We will appreciate what God has done that much more. We should keep in mind that ours is a "crock-pot redemption." God slowly, patiently works out his redemptive purposes over thousands of years and only "when the time had fully come" did God send his Son (Gal. 4:4). We would do well to pay attention to this gradual unfolding of his character and work so that we might savor his amazing grace and mercy even more.[5]

To summarize, we need to begin our interpretation by thinking first of what it meant for its original audience—reading front to back.[6] We ask the question, "What might the first readers have understood this text to mean *at that point in redemptive history?*" This reminds us that there is a progressiveness to God's revelation and we cannot ignore the specific context into which God's Word first comes.

Next, we reread the text in light of the *end* of the story— reading back to front. We *do* have to "go back to the future"! Ultimately, what is that future? The book of Revelation—the return of the King and the consummation of his kingdom—shows where history is going.

This "bidirectional" reading does justice to the unity *and* diversity of Scripture. We will listen for the particular voices and themes of individual books, but we also will pay attention to the ways they fit into the Bible as a whole and, more specifically, into the progressive plan of God's redemption.

2. Bigger Bible, Richer Ministry

It's clear that all parts of the Bible's story contribute their "voices" and therefore are fair game for use in ministry. Knowing that all parts of the Bible make their unique contribution to the whole gives us the courage and motivation to read and apply the Scriptures widely and deeply.

As we do, previously neglected parts of our Bibles—canyon passages—start to reveal themselves as integral parts of the story God is telling. We learn how to wrestle with the ways these passages relate to Christ and his church. It doesn't mean that it will always be easy! But it does encourage us to dig for the gospel connections that may not be apparent at first glance.

It also means that "tried and true" (ditch) passages take on new and deeper significance in light of the person and work of Jesus Christ. It doesn't mean that you won't use Ephesians 4:26–27 to counsel someone regarding her anger, but it does mean that you are more likely to connect that instruction to the gospel realities Paul lays out in the earlier verses of Ephesians, including 4:25: "we are all members of one body." And whose body is it? The body of Jesus Christ, the One who "himself is our peace, who has made the two [Jews and Gentiles] one and has destroyed the barrier, the dividing wall of hostility" (Eph. 2:14). Jesus himself brokers peace between enemies and makes them, at the cost of his own blood, part of his body. How much richer this is than merely talking about strategies to avoid sinful anger!

Perhaps you will still use the narrative of David and Goliath (1 Sam. 17) to encourage a struggling sister to press on against overwhelming adversity. But rather than simply highlighting David's courage and trust in his God, you can explore together the mysteries of a God who fights on behalf of his people but does so by taking on the weakness of human flesh and dying in seeming defeat on a cross. It appeared that "Goliath" got the victory after all, over Jesus, the Son of David. But no! Jesus Christ is the true King who rises in victory over the ultimate enemy—death. Your friend can draw comfort that, with death itself defeated, nothing can separate her from the love of Christ (Rom. 8:38–39), although she may continue to "groan" amid her present burdens (Rom. 8:18–25). Considering 1 Samuel 17 in this wider history of redemption reminds us that our lives in Christ are not always marked by the slaying of giants. We do experience a mix of suffering and triumph this side of glory.

3. The Centrality of God's Mission[7]

Seeing the Bible as a unified story of God's redemptive mission helps us avoid introspective, individualistic application. The endpoint of redemption isn't a redeemed and transformed individual life (your own or another's)—it is the restoration of *all* things! Have you caught that immense vision? Does it saturate your life and ministry? We can settle for too little in our use of Scripture, even when we genuinely look to the Scriptures to guide our lives. We are, to paraphrase C. S. Lewis, like children content to make mud pies in the backyard when a beach vacation is offered to them.[8] *Do* we keep before us the hope that "the earth will be filled with the knowledge of the glory of the LORD, as the waters cover the sea" (Hab. 2:14)?

Consider the way King Caspian stirred the courage and motivation of his weary sailors in Lewis's *The Voyage of the Dawn Treader.* In the midst of crew members debating the pros and cons of traveling further to the World's End, Caspian spoke:

> "Friends," he said, "I think you have not quite understood our purpose. You talk as if we had come to you with our hat in our hand, begging for shipmates. It isn't like that at all. We and our royal brother and sister and their kinsman and Sir Reepicheep, the good knight, and the Lord Drinian have an errand to the world's edge. It is our pleasure to choose from among such of you as are willing, those whom we deem worthy of so high an enterprise. We have not said that any can come for the asking. That is why we shall now command the Lord Drinian and Master Rhince to consider carefully what men among you are the hardest in battle, the most skilled seamen, the purest in blood, the most loyal to our person, and the cleanest of life and manners; and to give their names to us in a schedule." He paused and went on in a quicker voice: "Aslan's mane!" he exclaimed. "Do you think that the privilege of seeing the last things is to be bought for a song?"[9]

What motivates us to press on in faith when the adventure we signed up for has proven more difficult than we might have wished? If we view the gospel in shortsighted and individualistic terms—"Yeah, I know Jesus died for my sins, but what has he done for me *lately?*"—we are more tempted to grow cynical and self-absorbed. But if we view this life as colaboring with our King as "ministers of reconciliation" (2 Cor. 5:17–20), we are strengthened to press onward and outward, expressing our love for others in sacrificial ways. Do we set that expansive and glorious task before others?

For the New Testament authors, the "gospel" was the proclamation that the true King had come to claim his throne, with all its cosmic, corporate, *and* individual implications. Notice how

Paul describes the gospel in a nutshell in Galatians 3:8: "The Scripture foresaw that God would justify the Gentiles by faith, and announced the gospel in advance to Abraham: 'All nations will be blessed through you.'" No doubt, I am changed individually by this good news! But I am changed in order that, through Christ, I might be a blessing to others.

As we will see more fully in the next chapter, we were created to be a part of something bigger than ourselves. The Bible reveals the true story that is to capture our lives. We are ambassadors of the King, proclaiming to broken and sinful people the death and resurrection of Jesus Christ and his lordship over all creation until he comes again. Keeping this picture before us guards us from the temptation to use the Bible in "an attempt to come up with explanations or programs that fit the Holy Trinity into our Holy Needs, Holy Wants, and Holy Feelings."[10] It's easy to lose sight of the larger work God is doing in his creation when our own square foot of creation is in chaos. In the press of daily struggles, it's easy to become myopic and self-focused. This is precisely when the lordship of Christ and his mission to restore all things lift our weary heads. Part of the joy of ministry involves helping someone more consistently and richly live with the wide-angled lens of the Bible's redemptive plotline.

4. Bidirectional Living

There is a forward thrust to Scripture. Biblical theologians would call this an "eschatological" (moving toward "last things") impulse. This is because God is active in history, carrying out his redemptive agenda until Jesus returns. Although God's revelation to his people has ceased, God is still working in his world through his Spirit, his Word, and his church. So no matter where you are in Scripture, you should feel the inexorable pull forward to where history will end up.

At the same time, Scripture always points us backward to what God has done on behalf of his people. The Old Testament most often looks back to the exodus as the signal event of God's redemption. The New Testament, of course, points to Christ's death and resurrection as God's definitive redemptive event.

Interestingly, Titus 2:11–14 relates both the future and past elements to life in the present: "For the grace of God that brings salvation has appeared to all men [past]. It teaches us to say 'No' to ungodliness and worldly passions, and to live self-controlled, upright and godly lives in this present age [present], while we wait for the blessed hope—the glorious appearing of our great God and Savior, Jesus Christ [future], who gave himself for us [past] to redeem us from all wickedness and to purify for himself a people that are his very own, eager to do what is good [present]." This bi-directional dynamic—"What has God done already?" and "What does he have planned for the future?"—is modeled throughout Scripture.[11] Thus, we are people who constantly look backward and forward as we live our stories in the present. The Bible shows us that we cannot live as mere "present tense" Christians. Our present moments are framed by God's past acts of redemption and by the glorious future he has planned (1 Cor. 2:9–10).

5. Interpretation and Application as a Community Affair

Scripture is addressed to communities with few exceptions (3 John, possibly 2 John and Philemon). And even then, once these books are accepted as part of the Bible, they are recognized as sacred and authoritative writings for the church as a whole. One way to think about this is that the Bible is *his* (God's) story and *our* story before it is really *my* story.

This means that we should pursue interpretation and application of Scripture in dialogue with other believers, past and present. We should take seriously the interpretive endeavors and insights of believers around the world, not simply those who share the same skin color, language, or interpretive tradition. Does that sound risky to you? Perhaps it's far more risky to make the interpretation and use of Scripture into a monologue, or an "in-house" discussion where preconceived notions are never challenged, tested, reaffirmed, or set aside. I have interpretive blind spots that you (or, say, a Nigerian or Korean believer) might see more clearly—and vice versa. This is particularly important in personal ministry, which often occurs behind closed doors.

It also means that, when it comes to the transformation of life anticipated by the gospel, I *am* my brother's keeper. The plotline of the Bible envisions the church of Christ being ever transformed into his character. It's not simply a private affair in which I "get my life together" before God (as if that can ever happen!). Rather, because the Spirit of God, through the Word of God, is intent on building a community liberated and transformed by the gospel, I have "ministry eyes" for the people in my local church and beyond. I yearn to see my brothers and sisters and the church as a whole live in ways consistent with the reign of Jesus Christ.[12]

Bits without Bite?

In the last two chapters I have sought to build a case from Scripture that shows the Bible as the unfolding story of God's redemption. The question is, do you and I live in light of this grand story? Or do we choose bits and pieces of the Bible to structure bits and pieces of our lives, losing the comprehensive redemptive thrust of the gospel? Craig Bartholomew and Michael Goheen note the danger in doing so:

Many of us have read the Bible as if it were merely a mosaic of little bits—theological bits, moral bits, historical-critical bits, sermon bits, devotional bits. But when we read the Bible in such a fragmented way, we ignore its divine author's intention to shape our lives through its story. All human communities live out of some story that provides a context for understanding the meaning of history and gives shape and direction to their lives. If we allow the Bible to become fragmented, it is in danger of being absorbed into whatever *other* story is shaping our culture, and it will thus cease to shape our lives as it should. Idolatry has twisted the dominant cultural story of the secular Western world [and in reality, all human hearts!]. If as believers we allow this story (rather than the Bible) to become the foundation of our thought and action, then our lives will manifest not the truths of Scripture, but the lies of an idolatrous culture. Hence, the unity of Scripture is no minor matter: a fragmented Bible may actually produce theologically orthodox, morally upright, warmly pious idol worshippers![13]

This is one reason why the Bible so often strikes merely a glancing blow off our lives. Because we tend to use "bits" of the Bible for disconnected "bits" of daily life without paying attention to the whole, the whole of people's lives don't change. A dis-integrated Bible often leads to dis-integrated, compartmentalized lives. This doesn't mean we have to tell the whole story every time we minister the Word. Many conversations don't permit such depth. But it *does* mean that the sweeping, Christ-centered plotline of Scripture increasingly shapes the way we view and use any passage.

When we keep the story of God's kingdom front and center, we are more likely to view the totality of our lives, individually and corporately, as "fair game" for the Story's transformative power. As N. T. Wright says, "Tell someone to do something, and you change their life—for a day; tell someone a story and you change their life."[14]

Discussion Questions

1. Consider the Bible reading and study you did this week. Pick one passage and reflect on its place in the scope of God's redemption in history. How do the themes of your passage relate to what came before it and what comes after it? If it is an Old Testament passage consider, "How do the ideas and themes of this passage find their completion in Christ?" If it is a New Testament passage consider, "How do the themes of this passage find their anchor in Christ?"

2. Think of a time this week when you used a Scripture passage to minister to someone. Was the gospel central? Was the overarching story of Scripture part of the way you used the Bible? If not, how could you have done it differently?

3. What does your "intake" of Scripture look like? Do you have a reading plan? Do you tend toward reading larger chunks of Scripture or toward more focused study? Why might both

approaches be important outgrowths of taking the narrative structure of the Bible seriously?

4. Have you read the Bible from cover to cover? If not, what keeps you from doing so? If yes, do you continue that discipline on a regular basis?

5. What challenges or difficulties arise as you consider how to use Scripture in light of its overarching story?

CHAPTER 5

What's Your Story?

The last two chapters argued against a bits-and-pieces approach to the Bible and stressed instead the importance of reading the Bible as one story centering on the coming of Jesus Christ and his renewing rule. This larger, Christ-focused framework is what helps us understand the true significance of the diverse writings that make up the Bible.

But reading the Bible this way is only one side of the equation. To apply Scripture to our contemporary lives, we also need to understand people. We need to learn to "read" people wisely in order to embody the love and truth of Christ to them. Similar to my approach in the last two chapters, I want to give some overarching categories for understanding and approaching people. Getting the big picture will set us up to do more fine-grained work in succeeding chapters.

"Storied" Life

In ministry to others, it is easy to focus on bits and pieces, words and actions that are obvious to others: she yelled at her kids; he hooked up with a prostitute; she cheated on a math test; he gives sacrificially of his time and money to a local homeless shelter; she gave him the silent treatment; he faced the end of his life with dignity and hope. But what is the "narrative skeleton" on which those bits and pieces hang? Like the Bible, the details of our lives add up to a cohesive whole. Despite the diversity of thoughts, actions, emotions, words, situations, and relationships that make up our lives, certain patterns can be discerned. Life histories are going somewhere.

We all have a conception (even if we do so unawares) of how the various aspects of our lives—self-identity, relationships with God and others, experiences, events—relate to one another and give meaning and purpose to life.[1] We all have a grid for making sense of our experiences, a "North Star" by which we navigate life.

In this sense, everyone has a story. Not simply a story to tell but a story (or stories) to live, a plotline that is going somewhere. Or to use another metaphor, the trees *do* add up to a forest. Observing the details (trees) without discerning the overall pattern (forest) can lead to "ministerial meandering": getting lost in the details of someone's story without providing a biblical map that gives orientation, direction, and destination for the journey.

One of the key skills for a physician involves "taking a history" from a patient. This involves interviewing a patient intensively and extensively regarding several things: (1) the symptoms that brought him to the doctor or hospital ("history of the present illness"); (2) his past medical history; (3) his family history; (4) his social history, including tobacco, alcohol, or drug use; (5) his medications; and (6) the "review of systems," an extensive list of questions about other body systems besides the one(s) targeted in the history of the present illness. This structured interview is followed by a physical exam and perhaps several diagnostic tests.

Then comes a crucial question: what diagnostic possibilities do these details suggest? What patterns emerge from the information? Failure to discern the patterns in a patient's story can lead to delayed or wrong diagnosis, which can lead to delayed or wrong treatment. The goal of hearing a patient's story is not to assemble a list of details but to discern the medical plotline(s) that best explain and account for those details. This allows a physician to provide the best treatment for them.

In a similar way, if we are to be of real help to others, we need to carefully listen for the patterns that emerge from the details of their lives. They will give clues about how to bring the life-giving gospel to them. Listening to how people make sense of the details of their lives gives a sense of the overarching story or stories that guide their daily existence.

Worldview Questions

A way to speak about the storied quality of human life is to affirm that each person (or community) asks and answers foundational questions about the nature of life, consciously or subconsciously. The answers we give to these questions characterize our "worldview," our "take" on the nature of reality. The Bible itself answers these foundational questions and urges us to live in light of the biblical worldview, the true story of the world. In fact, you might say that even asking these questions shows that we are God's image bearers. As we will see later, the fact that we are broken, fallen image bearers means that we answer those questions in ways that compete with the biblical narrative.

Brian Walsh and J. Richard Middleton propose four basic worldview questions:[2]

1. Where are we? That is, what is the nature of the world in which we live?
2. Who are we? Or, what is the essential nature of human beings?
3. What's wrong? That is, why is the world (and my life!) in such a mess?
4. What's the remedy? Or, how can these problems be solved?

These questions—and how we answer them—form the narrative backbone of our lives. They shape the way we interpret life events, from the mundane (no milk in the refrigerator for the breakfast cereal) to the horrific (loss of children in a car accident). They shape our view of ourselves and others. They shape our vision of what constitutes a meaningful life, even a meaningful moment. They shape our beliefs, emotions, and decisions every day. Everybody has an overarching story he or she lives by, moment by moment.[3] Everybody is a meaning maker with categories for making sense of life. Reality does not come to us unfiltered but always through the lens of our perception. The real question is, What lens will we use? What story, what narrative will we use to see our world and interpret our lives?[4]

A Story from the Outside

Being made in the image of God includes a built-in interpretation of the nature of self and the world. In fact, it includes a built-in basic knowledge of God, of his "eternal power and divine nature" (Rom. 1:20). To be an image bearer is to have the Story imprint—God and his view of reality—upon you! To live in God's world is to be confronted daily with visible reminders of invisible realities (Rom. 1:19).

Notice that *even before* the fall of humanity into sin, Adam and Eve needed information about God and his world. They needed God's own "take" on his creation, a story line from outside themselves. And what were the elements of that story?[5] How did God give a framework of meaning and purpose for these newly minted human beings? Take a look at Genesis 1:28–30 and 2:15–17 to find out.

First, God gave them a *noble task:* multiply and rule the whole earth (Gen. 1:28). For Adam and Eve, being made in God's likeness meant bringing all of creation under God's rule. Their identity as God's image bearers was tightly wedded to a particular purpose, to live as stewards of God's creation.[6] The garden needed gardeners (Gen. 2:5–8)! Although I wouldn't consider myself an avid gardener, what gardening I do gives a profound sense of satisfaction as I cooperate with God in bringing order, beauty, and fruitfulness to my world.

Second, God gave them *freedom to eat* from seed-bearing plants and trees (Gen. 1:29). It reminded Adam and Eve that the Creator God had given this food to them; they were dependent on his generosity.

But third, although God gave them freedom, he did speak a negative word. He *prohibited them* from eating from the tree of the knowledge of good and evil. He warned them that if they disobeyed, they would die (Gen. 2:16–17).

So there it was. A simple story line. *Where are we?* "In a beautiful, perfect place created by God." *Who are we?* "We are God's own image bearers, unique among created things, who are to live in God's creation, bringing his rule to the ends of the earth. We are creatures who are to live under the wise authority of the Creator." That's the story by which Adam and Eve and their descendants were to live. But even in Paradise, a competing story line confronted them.

Competing Stories, Fallen People

While much could be said about the serpent's challenge to God, notice some of the places it cast doubt on God's instruction, added new information, or directly challenged God's authoritative story (Gen. 3:1–5). First the serpent misrepresented God as stingy: "Did God really say, 'You must not eat from any tree in the garden'?" (v. 1). Eve's answer was nearly right: "We may eat fruit from the trees in the garden, but God did say, 'You must not eat fruit from the tree that is in the middle of the garden, and you must not touch it, or you will die'" (vv. 2–3). Eve added to God's story line, saying that God also said "and you must not touch it [the forbidden fruit]." Now, either God said this and it's simply not noted in the Bible *or* (more likely) Eve gave her own elaboration to God's word.

In response, the serpent directly challenges God's story ("You will not surely die," v. 4) *and* adds some enticing details ("For God knows that when you eat of it your eyes will be opened, and you will be like God, knowing good and evil," v. 5).[7] Now Eve faces a choice: Whose story is most authoritative for her life? Which details matter? Whose word counts most?

Unfortunately, Eve chose the details that described a reality where humans were the pinnacle, where the rest of creation, and ultimately God himself, played a supporting role. And so when she "saw that the fruit of the tree was good for food and pleasing to the eye, and also desirable for gaining wisdom, she took some and ate it" (Gen. 3:6). In so doing, Adam and Eve effectively answered those first two worldview questions very differently. *Where are we?* "In a beautiful, perfect world where everything is ripe for the picking." *Who are we?* "We are independent creatures, free to choose whatever we think will bring us delight. We are creatures who can choose the path to Godlike wisdom. We have the power to discern good and evil." It's a very different take on reality, isn't it?

After that, things go downhill pretty fast as pain, toil, misery, sin, and death enter the world.[8] Since this first deviation from the true story of the universe, humanity has pursued alternate plotlines that exclude the authority of God's design for his creation and his people. Where does this lead? To Cain's slaying of Abel (Gen. 4:1–16). To Lamech's boasting (Gen. 4:19–24). And ultimately to the situation prior to the flood, where the Bible notes that "every inclination of the thoughts of his [mankind's] heart was only evil all the time" (Gen. 6:5). Power, greed, envy, elevation of self before others, blameshifting, vigilantism, injustice, and the like are the themes and practices of story lines that exclude God.

The third worldview question asks, "What's wrong?" The biblical answer is that we have chosen to live autonomously, by story lines of our own creation. We have rejected the idea that we are created worshipers of the living God and meant to image and glorify him in every aspect of our lives. We have embraced other identities, values, and purposes for life. Our thoughts, attitudes, emotions, and actions flow day by day out of these alternate plots. The result fits the description Paul uses in Titus 3:3: "At one time we too were foolish, disobedient, deceived and enslaved by all kinds of passions and pleasures. We lived in malice and envy, being hated and hating one another."

Fortunately, the early chapters of Genesis are not the end of the story! Scripture also provides an answer to the question, "What's the remedy for this mess?" Paul describes it like this: "But when the kindness and love of God our Savior appeared, he saved us, not because of righteous things we had done, but because of his mercy. He saved us through the washing of rebirth and renewal by the Holy Spirit, whom he poured out on us generously through Jesus Christ our Savior, so that, having been justified by his grace, we might become heirs having the hope of eternal life" (Titus 3:4–7).

God's mission for his people as stewards of his kingdom cannot be thwarted. God's story for his creation cannot be "re-authored," despite the powers of evil seeking to bring a premature and disastrous end to God's design. Rather, God himself will rescue his rebellious and sin-broken people by recreating a "new" people for himself (Israel), who will be a blessing to the nations (Gen. 12:2–3). As we saw in chapter 3, Israel's story and mission ultimately come to fulfillment in Jesus Christ. He, the perfect human and only Son of God, bears the punishment for our sin and is vindicated by his resurrection from the dead. Through the giving of the Holy Spirit, he creates the church, this band of kingdom people who will make disciples of all nations (Matt. 28:19–20), a new creation "echo" of Genesis 1:28.

The Story to Live By

So the issue is this: Will we answer the fundamental questions of life with the biblical story or some other story (or stories)? We *will* interpret the events of our lives with *some* overarching assumptions about the nature of ourselves and the world. The Bible is written to show us the true nature of reality. Scripture will either affirm or confront the stories by which we make sense of the details of our daily lives.

As a comprehensive story, the Bible answers the four questions that help us understand ourselves. These basic elements of the story—creation, fall, redemption, and consummation—will shape our worldview. As Richard Harris notes, "A worldview provides the loom for weaving the tapestry of understanding out of the strings of experience."[9] Again, the question is, what "loom" are we using to organize the threads of our experience?

It's easy to say that we are "living by God's story" in some abstract way. But when there is an obvious disconnect between the biblical vision for life and the features of our own lives (which occurs daily, right?!), we must pause and ask, "What alternative stories, interpretations of life, and beliefs are we *really* living under?" These competing stories guarantee that personal ministry is necessary. Ministry is about helping others see the story lines by which they are living. But what does this look like in practice?

Discovering the Stories by Which We Live . . . or Die

Let me illustrate this with a common experience: family dissension on vacation! Not long ago, our family stayed for a week in a cottage on the southern Maine coast. It was April, so we were expecting colder weather. What we didn't expect was the biggest snowstorm of the season, which knocked out power and water for two days. Interestingly, two of us were not especially deterred in our enthusiasm while the other two (who shall remain nameless!) found what amounted to "indoor camping" less than desirable. (Truth be told, we all wearied of boiling snow for water eventually!)

Now, why did the very same series of events result in one group of people responding one way—taking the challenges in stride, not so much bothered with the lack of showers—and another group responding a different way—grumbling and complaining, wanting to leave early? It was because the complainers in our family were living by a different story line than the more contented members. A functionally different worldview guided the two groups. If we were honest, here's how each pair might have answered the fundamental worldview questions noted above. (OK, with a *bit* of exaggeration!)

The Complainers
- *Where are we?* We are on a well-deserved vacation in a place designed to meet our needs.
- *Who are we?* We are the center of our universe. All of creation is meant to serve us! Nothing matters but our comfort.
- *What's wrong?* This stupid snowstorm is ruining everything. We expected comfort, relaxation, and no stress.
- *What's the solution?* We need to escape this nightmare, and we will keep complaining until we do.

The Contented
- *Where are we?* We are on vacation in a beautiful part of God's creation.

- *Who are we?* We are servants of God, called to live out the kingdom values of Jesus Christ wherever we are. We are people who are redeemed, yet await the full redemption that Jesus will bring when he returns.
- *What's wrong?* Something we didn't expect has happened and revealed how demanding and self-centered we are tempted to be. This unexpected situation still exists under the reign of our wise and loving Father. It's also true that, in this time between the first and second comings of Jesus, suffering and hardship are part of the norm of Christian living, as Romans 8:18–23 notes.
- *What's the solution?* Embrace the snowstorm as God's fatherly design, enjoy the beauty of the snow, ask God for his help in moving from disappointment to contentment, *and* wisely assess whether it would be better to leave early if we can't shower or flush the toilets!

Notice how different the overarching stories are that guide the responses of both groups! Notice that the complainers use a self-oriented lens to view events and respond accordingly. The more contented group uses a biblical lens to place the same events within God's larger redemptive story.

This same battle plays out each day in your lives as well. Every time you are harsh with your children, every time you use words to manipulate your spouse, every time you turn the other way when you could have offered assistance, you reveal the self-oriented story you are living by. And every time you choose not to repay evil for evil, every time you welcome the outsider to your fellowship, every time you give yourself in costly sacrifice to your spouse, you reveal the God-oriented story that guides your life. If you're like me, the switch from a God-authored to a self-authored script can happen in an instant!

In our ministry to people we need to notice how the details of their lives point to larger worldviews. As you get to know them, ask the kinds of questions that reveal their motives and thoughts about God, others, themselves, and the world. Acknowledging how hard it is for *us* to live consistently by God's story keeps us humble as we identify the competing stories of those we serve.

Approaching People as Saints, Sufferers, and Sinners

The Bible does more than lay out a broad story line by which to live. It does more than stay at the level of the worldview questions we just considered. It tailors the contours of the story to people who need to hear how God's redemptive acts impact all aspects of daily life. Geerhardus Vos concurs: "All that God disclosed of Himself has come in response to the practical religious needs of His people as these emerged in the course of history."[10] And how does God speak to his people in response to their needs? He shapes his story to approach his people as saints, sufferers, and sinners.[11]

Why is it important to highlight these aspects of our identity as believers? They describe our experience before Jesus returns to consummate his kingdom. How we live in our "roles" as saints, sufferers, and sinners reveals how aligned we really are with God's Word. Whether or not people are living out their identity as sons or daughters of God reveals how close or far they are from God's redemptive plotline. How people grapple with the nature and purpose of suffering this side of heaven reveals whether or not (in the moment at least) they are living in line with God's overarching story. And how individuals own and act on the sin in their lives also reveals how committed they remain to the details of God's Word.

Another way of saying this is that each person we meet is wrestling in some way with two problems. First, the problem of identity and purpose: who am I and what in the world should I be doing? (This corresponds to God's address to us as saints.) Second, the problem of evil: evil from "without" (which corresponds to our experience as sufferers) and evil from "within" (which corresponds to our experience as sinners).

Where do we see these distinctions of saint, sufferer, and sinner in Scripture? Notice that these categories are always operating in us simultaneously and implicitly. But a given passage of Scripture often explicitly highlights just one of these aspects. There are passages that more specifically focus on the identity of God's people or comfort the afflicted or deal with issues of sin in the lives of believers. Let's take a closer look.

Saint

First, the very existence of God's Word presupposes the "saint" distinction. God's Word comes to *his* chosen and beloved people, the descendants of Abraham, Isaac, and Jacob; and it comes to those Gentiles who have been engrafted into Israel's story (Rom. 11). No doubt the term *saint* finds its fullest expression in the work of Christ—we are saints (literally, "holy" or "set apart" ones) who have been sanctified ("made holy") in Jesus Christ (1 Cor. 1:2; 6:11), but throughout Scripture God addresses his people as those who are set apart for him.

God often explicitly reminds his people who they are. These statements abound in Scripture. Let me highlight a few:[12]

- We are image bearers of the one true God (Gen. 1:26).
- We are those to whom and through whom the blessing of the nations has come (Gen. 12:2–3; Gal. 3:8–9).
- We are part of the community God chose and took for himself (Deut. 4:32–40).
- We are those who are distinguished by the very presence of God (Exod. 33:16).
- We are sanctified and justified in Christ Jesus (1 Cor. 1:2; 6:11).
- We are chosen, redeemed, forgiven children of God in Christ, who have been given the Holy Spirit (Eph. 1:3–14; Gal. 4:6–7).
- We are "a chosen people, a royal priesthood, a holy nation, a people belonging to God" (see 1 Pet. 2:4–11).[13]

Notice how closely connected the identity of God's people is to God himself. We are defined by our relationship with him! In a world that beckons people to define themselves by false and fading identities based on looks, intelligence, wealth, power, or success, this is good news! Unlike worldly definitions of identity, our identity and inheritance in Christ never fades (1 Pet. 1:3–4). In our Bible reading, we should be on the lookout for how God's Word addresses us as saints, as people set apart for our good and his glory. This will prepare us to speak to people who may have forgotten who they really are!

Sufferer

What about the "role" of sufferer? Again, Scripture assumes that, since the fall, the people God has chosen *are* sufferers. They are constantly faced with evils from outside themselves. Here are a few places where this is clear in Scripture:

- The exodus from Egypt. Exodus 3:7–8 is particularly instructive: "The LORD said, 'I have indeed seen the misery of my people in Egypt. I have heard them crying out because of their slave drivers, and I am concerned about their suffering. So I have come down to rescue them from the hand of the Egyptians.'"
- In Judges you see the Israelites crying out to God for deliverance from the oppression of foreign nations. We hear that "the LORD had compassion on them as they groaned under those who oppressed and afflicted them" (Judg. 2:18). Interestingly, these early chapters also reveal that God himself was the one who handed his people over to their enemies because of Israel's idolatry. In Judges (and throughout Scripture), sin and suffering are intertwined. You don't see an artificial wedge between the two. God takes sin seriously, and God takes suffering seriously (even when the suffering stems from sinful choices!). God is compassionate toward sinners who suffer because of their own sin. He doesn't shrug his shoulders indifferently toward the wayward and oppressed Israelites, as if to say, "I told you so."
- The psalmists (especially in lament psalms such as 13, 22, 44, 88, and others) cry out to God in their misery, expecting his intervention, for God "has not despised or disdained the suffering of the afflicted one; he has not hidden his face from him but has listened to his cry for help" (Ps. 22:24).
- God calls to account those who oppress and perpetrate injustice upon others (Jer. 23; Ezek. 34; Amos).
- Paul notes that this life involves "groaning" in the midst of suffering (Rom. 8:18–27).

- The books of Hebrews, 1 Peter, and Revelation are written to suffering communities, giving hope, perspective, and direction in the midst of their suffering and persecution.

It is clear from Scripture that suffering is a significant thread that runs through the story of God's people. In Jesus and because of his resurrection, the saints long for the time when "there will be no more death or mourning or crying or pain" and God "will wipe every tear from their eyes" (Rev. 21:4). But meanwhile, believers suffer as people united to their Savior, who endured suffering prior to *his* glory.[14]

Sinner

Thirdly, consider the aspect of living as a sinner. Scripture assumes that its hearers and readers *need* redemption since humanity's fall into sin. The Bible presupposes that we are faced incessantly with evils from *within* ourselves. Sin's pervasive reality is like gravity that continually pulls the people of God downward. It should prompt the question Paul asks: "Who will rescue me from this body of death?" (Rom. 7:24). Ultimately, nothing but the sacrifice of Christ can redeem sinners (Heb. 7:26–27 and elsewhere in Hebrews; 2 Cor. 5:21).

Every page of the Bible is addressed implicitly to sinners, but here are several places where the gravity and insanity of sin stare us full in the face.

- "The LORD saw how great man's wickedness on the earth had become, and that every inclination of the thoughts of his heart was only evil all the time" (Gen. 6:5).
- In Leviticus, the sacrificial system was a multisensory reminder of the reality and wages of sin. Sinners seeking restoration with God would hear the cry of the slaughtered animal, see the crimson stain, feel the slip and stick of blood, and smell the burning sacrifice. There was no getting around the seriousness of breaking God's law, even unintentionally.

- The book of Judges highlights that "everyone did as he saw fit" (Judg. 21:25) and records one of the most horrific acts in all Scripture (Judg. 19).
- First and Second Kings reveal the dissolution of the Davidic/Solomonic kingdom into Israel and Judah and narrate the inexorable slide of God's people into idolatry, leading to the destruction of both nations. Experiencing the consequences of their sins did not dissuade them from their rebellion (see Amos 4).
- Only the intervention of God himself—a heart transplant!—can cure his people of their backsliding (Jer. 3, especially 3:22; Ezek. 36:24–32; 37).

You might say that such a dismal picture of sin and its consequences is appropriate for the Old Testament, but what about the New Testament? Didn't Jesus conquer sin? Hasn't the age of the Spirit dawned? Yes, but the New Testament also teaches that we live in the "overlap of the ages," the time between Jesus' resurrection and his return. Through Jesus, the age to come has broken into this present evil age (Gal. 1:3–4). He gives us his Spirit as the "firstfruits" of God's new creation, guaranteeing that we *will* experience the full harvest of redemption, including resurrection (Rom. 8:23; Eph. 1:13–14). Although redemption has already been accomplished through Jesus Christ, it is not yet fully realized for God's people (Phil. 3:12–14). Continued struggle with sin—war between flesh and Spirit—characterizes our living in the overlap of the ages.

Clearly, the New Testament epistles reveal that new life in Christ was by no means "automatic." God's people struggled with the continued presence of sin.[15] They needed instruction, confrontation, encouragement, and warning. The New Testament writers proclaimed the finished work of Christ, but they also affirmed the challenge of applying that finished work to daily life. Every church continued to wrestle with competing stories about where identity, meaning, and purpose were found. Every group of believers struggled to close the gap between the indicatives and the imperatives of the gospel. Each church grappled with how to see and do life through the new eyes the gospel gave.

That ongoing struggle was the womb for the personal ministry of the apostles and New Testament writers! We, too, have the privilege of helping people identify and forsake the siren songs of the world, the flesh, and the devil.

To conclude, the Bible speaks to our experiences as saints, sufferers, and sinners. God's redemptive words *confirm* our identity as the chosen people of God, *console and comfort* his afflicted people, and *confront* the ways we turn away from his character and redemptive work. The worldview the Scriptures present is not depersonalized, as if we could ask the four worldview questions in abstraction. Rather, we are meant to enter into the story of God in the very personal experiences of life lived as saints, sufferers, and sinners. As we'll see in the next chapters, our use of Scripture must have that same multifaceted nature.

Ignorance Is Not Bliss!

What happens in ministry if we ignore these broad categories for understanding people? If we miss the fact that people have a dominant story (or stories) that shapes and directs the course of their lives, ministry will look a lot like putting out multiple brushfires. Have you experienced that? Stamping out a fire one week only to find the hose is needed again the following week? Why is that? Without considering the shaping stories of people's lives, we'll provide solution-focused counsel but perhaps miss the roots of the problem. We will use a weed-whacker rather than pull up stubborn problems by their roots! This is not to say that troubleshooting is a bad thing. In fact, in crisis situations (e.g., domestic violence or suicidal threats) I'm not necessarily asking about shaping stories; I take action to preserve life and dig deeper later. But as a whole, if we don't recognize people's functional worldviews, we won't make much sense of the thoughts, attitudes, words, and actions that flow out of their overarching stories. People don't need compartmentalized solutions for compartmentalized problems. They need the liberating story of redemption that gradually reunites the various aspects of their lives to be in line with gospel truth.

If we fail to consider the category of "saint," we will be tempted to focus entirely on the "not yet" aspect of people's lives.

Rather than celebrate the marks of redemption already present, we will focus on what they still lack. I think about this as a parent. It's appropriate for me to point out my children's sin and encourage them to repent. It's appropriate to train them to live differently, in line with biblical truth. But here's the rub: I catch them doing things *wrong,* but do I catch them doing something *right?!* Do I affirm where I see the Spirit at work in their lives? How often do I tell them how glad I am to be their father? As we will see in chapter 7, Paul does this with his spiritual children frequently. If we don't model our ministry with that same emphasis, affirming identity in Christ and the fruit of the Spirit in people's lives, they may become discouraged, unmotivated, or just plain angry.

What happens if we ignore the category of "sufferer" in people we serve? We will be insensitive to the relational and circumstantial challenges people face. We will minimize sin committed against them and maximize sin they commit. In our zeal to call people to account for their sin, we will overlook injustice done to them. We will miss the ways they experience the pain of their problems. Bottom line, we will miss their cry for help.

I'll never forget one of the early counseling classes I took with Paul Tripp. We watched a videotaped first session with a very angry, blameshifting man. Our assignment for the next week was to consider how we might approach this man. I figured that I had one shot with this guy. I suspected that no matter what I said, he would resist my counsel and would not return for another appointment. So I let him have it with both barrels (on paper, at least!). I lobbed mortar after mortar of biblical truth to blow up his self-oriented ways of living. *Not bad,* I thought. *Maybe he'll take what I've said and the Spirit will use it later.* Then I returned to class to hear Paul speak about the importance of connecting with this man's pain as a first step to help him. "Otherwise, he may never return," he said. Ouch! Guilty as charged! It's not that this man didn't have sin issues, but the first priority was to connect with his experience as a sufferer. Remember, most people seek help because they are suffering and need hope.

Lastly, if we minimize the category of "sinner," we water down the reality that people are responsive and responsible image bearers. Jeremiah's indictment will be true of us: "They dress the wound of my people as though it were not serious. 'Peace, peace,' they say, when there is no peace" (Jer. 6:14; also 8:11). We do people no favors when we overlook their self-destructive (and others-destructive) patterns. God's design is that his children might increasingly reflect the character of Christ. Peter captures it well: "As obedient children, do not conform to the evil desires you had when you lived in ignorance. But just as he who called you is holy, so be holy in all you do; for it is written: 'Be holy, because I am holy'" (1 Pet. 1:14–16). Our adoption as sons and daughters means that we act in keeping with our royal inheritance. Real faith produces tangible change, as the book of James notes (2:14–17).

You can see that all three perspectives are critical for balanced ministry. This is not to say that we can know anyone exhaustively nor that we have to flesh out these categories fully before we can move into someone's life. But they serve as touchstones of human experience that guide our efforts to understand people.

Time to Connect

Over the last three chapters, I have given a broad overview for reading the Bible and reading people. Now I want to consider how to bring these two readings together. How *do* we practically connect the narrative of the gospel with the narrative of people's lives? How does God's story engage us fully in our experience as saints, sufferers, and sinners? That is the direction of the second half of the book.

Discussion Questions

1. When someone shares with you the joys and difficulties of life, what overarching categories do you use to understand the details of that person's life?
2. Consider your own life and the lives of those you are serving. What competing stories (interpretations of reality) threaten to drown out the all-encompassing perspective of God's Word? (It may help to revisit the four worldview questions.)

3. What hinders you when you seek to bring God's redemptive message into your life? Into others' lives?
4. Which of the three aspects of our experience—saint, sufferer, and sinner—do you most identify with? Why?
5. Which of the three aspects do you find easiest to address in those you serve? Why? What hinders balance in your approach?

CHAPTER 6

Connecting the Stories

W e've talked about reading Scripture as an unfolding story of redemption that climaxes in Christ. We've discussed reading people in a way that recognizes the overarching stories of their lives. Now let's turn to the task of connecting Scripture to individual lives. This is where we seek to bridge the gap between then and now, whether the gap seems as large as a canyon or as small as a ditch. I'll begin with some general guidelines for using the Bible in ministry.

Using Scripture in Personal Ministry[1]

There are several overarching things to remember as we seek to connect the biblical story to the stories of people.

1. Some Passages Speak More Clearly to Certain Issues Than Others, but All Passages Provide a Lens through Which to View Any Issue

For example, Luke 12:22–34 speaks specifically to the problem of worry and fear, while 1 Peter 1:3–9 (which describes God's redemptive mercies as the reason to persevere in the midst of persecution) does not. Yet I have used both passages to minister to an anxious person. Luke 12's "antidote" to fear is grounded in verse 32: "Do not be afraid, little flock, for your Father has been pleased to give you the kingdom," a possession that can never be taken away, no matter what. Using the 1 Peter passage, we would highlight the living hope we have through Christ's resurrection and the imperishable inheritance that awaits us. Ultimately we taste a bit of that future now in Christ, and that is how we deal with hardship-provoked anxiety in the present.

As another example, in ministering to a couple in conflict, we could use James 4:1–11, which begins with the question, "What causes fights and quarrels among you?" Or we could use 1 Peter 2:9–10, which does not discuss relational conflict at all but describes the identity of believers using language reminiscent of Israel. With James we would highlight how relational conflict is ultimately rooted in one's attitude toward the Lord and urge each person to sift his or her motives and desires before God. In using 1 Peter, we could invite the couple to wrestle with the relational implications of being part of the people of God, as a chosen people, a royal priesthood, and a holy nation.

2. In Ministry to Others, We Move from Life to Text *or* Text to Life

What does it mean to move from "life to text"? Here we are asking what themes and pastoral needs are present in the life of the person we hope to help. Then we consider what passage(s) may address those needs. We pick a passage we think would resonate with this person in the midst of his struggles. For example, we might choose Luke 12 or Philippians 4:5–7 for an anxious person. For someone who struggles to forgive others we might choose Matthew 18:21–35 (the parable of the unmerciful servant) or Colossians 3:12–14. We look for a passage that speaks more specifically to the problem. This is similar to preaching a sermon that is focused on a particular topic such as marriage or money, with the preacher choosing texts that speak directly to the issue.

But we also want to grow in our ability to move from "text to life." Let's say that I have been struck by a particular text, perhaps through personal study, and I choose to use this passage with someone I am mentoring or counseling. This would be the equivalent of expository preaching, with the preacher working his way through a book of the Bible and making applications to his listeners' lives as he goes. Essentially, the text provides the "raw ingredients" for the ministry encounter, and I ask myself, "How can I best prepare a meal for this particular person?" When counseling others, it is not uncommon for me to use a single passage that has been particularly meaningful to me with several people in a given day! I may highlight different aspects of the passage with different people, but the initial "ministry move" has been from text to life.

In one-on-one ministry, we are more likely to choose life to text. As we hear the details of a person's life, certain themes emerge that, by the Spirit's prompting, suggest certain relevant biblical themes and passages. Typically, as I prepare for counseling, I prayerfully consider what direction a particular session ought to take and what facet of the gospel a counselee most needs to hear. Certain passages, familiar to me from previous use or study, come to mind. I may or may not end up using these passages based on the direction of the conversation, but I keep them in mind.

However, one danger of moving exclusively in this direction (from life to text) is that we can end up with a limited arsenal of ditch passages. We may be more prone to proof-texting and to offering superficial principles and advice. But if we put the passage we choose into the larger context of God's unfolding redemptive story, it should guard us from a simplistic, proof-text approach. Remember, I'm not arguing against the use of ditch passages per se. Nor am I arguing against deriving principles from a text, particularly if the ancient and modern ministry situations are comparable. Rather, I want our use of such passages and principles to remain connected to the larger story of God.

3. Some Passages *Are* More Easily Used in Ministry Situations Than Others

That is, the gap between the world of the text and the present situation is more easily bridged. For example, if I'm going to open up a passage to a couple in marital conflict, I may well use Ephesians 5:21–33 or Philippians 2:1–11, both of which have clear relational implications. It is much less likely that I would use 1 Chronicles 1—9, the genealogy of Jewish exiles returning to Palestine! The more difficult passages, if we use them, will likely provide a more general perspective on the problems at hand. What we identify as "easier" (ditch) passages are likely to be more specifically oriented to the problem at hand, which, of course, is why they are easier to apply!

But I know what you're thinking: *How* would *I "apply" 1 Chronicles 1—9 in a marriage counseling situation?* OK, here goes! Chronicles is likely written for the Jews who had returned to Judea after the exile (and/or their descendants).[2] They may well have been questioning their connection with the past work and promises of God. The genealogy reminds them of the connection that still exists, going all the way back to Adam. In itself, it reminded them of God's relentless, passionate work to preserve his people, despite their intentions to live by other plotlines. Ultimately, God's redemption and preservation center on Jesus Christ. Today he includes this warring husband and wife in the one beloved people of God. Hopefully, the worldview for this husband and wife, which has shrunk to the suffocating confines of their disappointments and bickering, will expand a bit as they see that God has swept them up into his grand story. Just as the returning Jews faced head-on the challenges of rebuilding Jerusalem, confident of God's faithfulness despite their sin, so can this couple move toward each other to rebuild their marriage, confident of God's faithfulness expressed through Jesus Christ. Shouldn't these redemptive realities give this couple a reason to pause before they strike out at each other?

So, we could use both Ephesians 5 and 1 Chronicles 1—9 to minister to this couple, but the latter will provide a more general perspective (and will require the counselor to do a bit more interpretive "leg work" to show its relevance to their lives). This raises a question: Just because I *could* use 1 Chronicles 1—9 to minister to this couple, *should* I? The short answer is no, probably not. You have to use wisdom in the moment. Unless the couple has some familiarity with 1 Chronicles, it may require too much time to "set up" the passage for use. I don't want the journey to eclipse the destination! Using this passage may feel too "cerebral" in the midst of an emotionally charged situation. I don't want people politely nodding their heads as we discuss a passage. I want to do everything I can to engage them. For these reasons, I can think of many other passages I would use instead of 1 Chronicles 1—9.

So, what's the point? What I'm trying to do is to push you a bit, to encourage you to get out of familiar ruts. I want you to see that more difficult (canyon) passages still apply to our lives. I don't want you to write off the first nine chapters of 1 Chronicles as irrelevant for today. As I mentioned earlier, I want your Bible to "grow" in its applicability. Of course, I want you to exercise wisdom as you make decisions about what theme or passage may be most helpful for particular people. The less familiar someone is with the Bible, the more likely we are to use short passages where the main points are more clear and the life connections are more immediate.

4. Major on Connections That Arise from the Passage as a Whole, Not So Much on Isolated Phrases

The larger the chunk of text, the better and more natural the connections. Biblical scholars stress that meaning lies at least at the sentence level, if not at the level of larger chunks of discourse.[3] This is not to say that the details and individual words of a passage don't matter. Often, it's only in a close study of the details that the significance of the whole passage comes to light. Those details may be what connect with the person's life, but it still needs to happen as you understand the theme(s) of the whole passage.

5. Remember That All Passages Are Linked in Some Way to Jesus Christ and His Redemptive Work

Each text reveals a particular facet of the unfolding story that moves—forward or backward—toward the coming(s) of Jesus Christ. As we saw earlier, this Christ-oriented trajectory of Scripture heightens its applicability to us. By virtue of our union with *the* Word, Jesus Christ (John 1:1, 14), we drink from the same stream of revelation as did earlier generations of God's people. But let me add two cautions.

Not every passage speaks *explicitly* about Christ. The details of a text do not necessarily have detailed Christological significance. In other words, we should beware of making gospel connections in a fanciful, allegorical way. Consider the example of Augustine. In a sermon on Proverbs 31:10–31, Augustine sees the woman as a symbol for the church. Accordingly, he approaches the text looking for the meaning as it relates to Christ or to the church. For example, he interpreted "she gets up while it is still dark" (v. 15) as the tribulations of the church. The "lamp" of verse 18 represents Christian hope. The "linen and purple" of verse 22 he saw as the two natures of Christ.[4] I don't know about you, but that's not what *I* thought of when I read those verses. What should we think of this approach?

On the one hand we should applaud the gospel lens that Augustine and other early church fathers used to interpret any passage of Scripture.[5] However, that approach should not overlook the original intent of the biblical author. Christ-centered and church-centered interpretations of Scripture are linked in some way to the original purposes for which God spoke redemptively. I hope that the remainder of this chapter and the next provide some responsible guardrails against overly complex, fanciful connections to Christ and the church.[6]

As a second caution, consider the story Graeme Goldsworthy tells of an Australian Sunday school teacher who thought she was being too predictable in her teaching and in the kinds of questions she asked. She decided to change her approach. The next Sunday she asked her five-year-old class, "Who can tell me what is gray and furry and lives in a gum (or eucalyptus) tree?" The children were surprised by the question and thought it must be a trick question, so they stared blankly at the teacher. "Come on," she coaxed. "Someone must know. What is gray, furry, lives in a gum tree, has a black leathery nose and beady eyes?" Still no answer. Finally a little girl raised her hand. "Yes, Suzie?" the teacher said. The child replied, "I know the answer is Jesus, but it sounds like a Koala!"[7]

We should beware of making overly simplistic, predictable connections so that the answer to any question about any passage is "Jesus"! One critique of the redemptive-historical approach to the Scriptures is that it "flattens" the contours and details of the Word. Goldsworthy's point is well taken. Yet I want to affirm that in our approach to Scripture and to people, we must do justice to *both* the diversity and the unity of the Bible's plotline. In later chapters, I hope you will see that such balance is possible.

Bottom line: Remember that every text is part of God's revelation that reaches its climax in the coming(s) of Christ. Thus, every passage must be understood ultimately *in relation to* the coming of the kingdom in Jesus, even if the details of a text don't explicitly map onto him. We should not overly complicate a text by allegorizing, nor should we overly simplify a text by connecting it to Jesus in some generic way.

A Diagram of the Approach

Here is a diagram of the approach I'm suggesting, which I'll flesh out in greater depth in the next chapter.

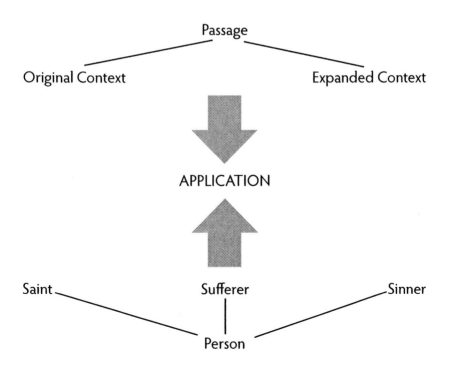

In ministry we are reading two "texts" simultaneously, the story of Scripture and the story of the person we serve. In ministry we must always have one eye on the biblical text and one eye on the individual. Or better, our gaze constantly shifts between the two. Reading the Bible without reading the person is a recipe for irrelevance in ministry. Reading the person without reading the Bible is a recipe for ministry lacking the life-changing power of the Spirit working through his Word.

When we read Scripture, we notice details that reveal the pastoral intentions of a text for its original audience ("original context"). We also expect to see how the themes of the passage relate to the rest of the Bible and, most particularly, to the climax of redemption in Christ ("expanded context"). When we read people, we are attentive to the details of their lives. We discover how these details fit into their experience as saints, sufferers, and sinners. This helps us understand the God-centered or self-centered story lines by which they live.

Our ultimate goal is application, the place where these two readings come together to bear good fruit—greater love for God and for others. Application happens when people "inhabit" the worldview of the text in such a way that they gain gospel-centered clarity and direction for their situation—and act on it. This is what connecting Scripture and life is all about! The goal of reading Scripture is not merely to produce an accurate, detailed outline of the passage. Nor is it simply to gain an understanding of how a text might have impacted its original audience. Nor is it a whiz-bang, jaw-dropping, creative connection of the passage to the person and work of Christ. Nor is it to generate a list of action steps to take. Similarly, the goal of reading people does not stop with understanding the particulars of their lives as saints, sufferers, and sinners. Those insights alone will not bring change. Rather, the goal of reading Scripture and reading people *together* is so that we can help others increasingly reflect the character and kingdom priorities of Jesus Christ. The goal of connecting Scripture with life is nothing less than changed lives, a changed community, and a changed world, as people listen to the God who speaks truth and love. This is *CrossTalk* in action!

In the next chapter I will offer some questions you can ask about the Bible passage at hand or about the person you are serving to encourage these redemptive connections.

Discussion Questions

1. How might you use Philippians 4:5–7 to minister to an anxious person? How might you use Psalm 77?
2. How would you use James 1:19–27 to minister to an angry person? How might you use Psalm 77?
3. What passage of Scripture has recently caught your attention? Why is it meaningful to you? Consider how you might use this passage in the lives of two people you know.
4. Think of a person you are ministering to now. What themes stand out in her life? Brainstorm five potential Bible passages you might use to connect the truth of Scripture with her life. Ask yourself, "What was it about these passages that led me to choose them for this person?"

CHAPTER 7
An In-Depth Look
at the Model

Let's turn now to some specific questions you can use to imple-
ment the model from the previous chapter. These questions
will help you understand the person and help you understand the
biblical text as you move toward application.

But first, let me address some concerns you might have as
you read this chapter. I suspect that you may feel overwhelmed
at the thought of using the questions in actual ministry settings.
You may feel like ministry in the moment does not permit such
in-depth study of the person or the Bible. And you may be right!
I'm certainly not asking you to keep someone waiting for an hour
while you plow through these questions! How then, should the
questions help you? Let me offer several metaphors: musical, ath-
letic, and culinary.

Think about the use of Scripture in ministry as an accordion. Sometimes the musician stretches out the accordion as far
as it can go; other times he or she compresses it together. Making music involves expansion, then contraction, expansion, then
contraction. Ministry is a lot like that too. Sometimes we have
only five or ten minutes with a person. Our opportunity is *contracted*, and we do what we can to listen and understand. We do
what we can to bring a biblical perspective to his struggles, even
if it only involves reading a verse or two without much comment.

We may point out one relevant aspect of the text. Or we may not turn to a specific verse at all but simply listen or pray. Other ministry opportunities are *expanded* over days, weeks, and months. These ongoing relationships provide the potential for an ever-growing understanding of the person coupled with an in-depth use of Scripture. Think of the questions that follow as helpful ways to prepare for those extended opportunities. (Although I think you'll find that keeping them in mind enriches the more contracted opportunities as well.)

Second, consider these questions (particularly the ones related to Scripture) as training that prepares you for game day. An athlete's hard work between games increases the chance of a top performance in the heat of competition. I would urge you to make the "Questions to Help You Understand the Passage" part of your regular Bible study. As you approach Scripture through the lens of these questions, you will be more prepared for a ministry encounter in which God may bring your previous study and insights to mind. Remember, you can't point out to others what you haven't seen yourself.

Third, I see these questions as the ingredients for a gourmet meal. But often in ministry you may have time only for a "quick bite"! You don't have to know the answers to all these questions in depth to prepare a nutritious meal for the person you serve. In fact, you may only have the opportunity to provide a hearty snack (e.g., focusing on a biblical character's posture toward God). But the more practiced you become in approaching Scripture and people as guided by the questions, the easier it will be to serve a feast when the time seems right.

Finally, view these questions as invitations to relationship with God and with others. The questions should lead you to a personal knowledge of God (through his Word) and people, which the Spirit brings together in life-changing ways.

Questions to Help You Understand the Person

The following questions are not necessarily ones you would ask someone directly (although some could be used that way). Think of them as ways to organize information as you get to know people. They will help you get a sense of how their lives "answer" the four worldview questions mentioned in chapter 5. Let's make use of the three biblical categories the Bible uses to describe people: saint, sufferer, and sinner.

Questions for the Saint

Here are two questions to consider:

1. What evidence of God's grace do you see in the person's life?
2. In what ways do you see the individual already living true to her identity in Christ? (That is, how does the person already exhibit the character of Christ in word and deed?)[1]

Why begin here? It's important to look for evidence of God's redemption in people's lives. Ministry to others is much more than correction or reproof. It is also encouragement ("Here's where I see Jesus already at work in your life"), vision-casting, and hope-building.

Think about the way Paul addressed the Corinthian church, a church so full of problems that he had to write at least two letters about their issues. Yet notice how he starts in 1 Corinthians 1:2: "To the church of God in Corinth, to those sanctified in Christ Jesus and called to be holy." In verses 4–9, he says, "I always thank God for you because of his grace given you in Christ Jesus. For in him you have been enriched in every way— in all your speaking and in all your knowledge—because our testimony about Christ was confirmed in you. Therefore you do not lack any spiritual gift as you eagerly wait for our Lord Jesus Christ to be revealed. He will keep you strong to the end, so that you will be blameless on the day of our Lord Jesus Christ. God, who has called you into fellowship with his Son Jesus Christ our Lord, is faithful." These verses are chock-full of identity statements—this is who they are—and assertions of how God has been at work in their midst. Then, and only then, does he discuss their problems.

We also see this focus in 6:9–10: "Do you not know that the wicked will not inherit the kingdom of God? Do not be deceived: Neither the sexually immoral nor idolaters nor adulterers nor male prostitutes nor homosexual offenders nor thieves nor the greedy nor drunkards nor slanderers nor swindlers will inherit the kingdom of God." This stern warning is in keeping with what he said earlier in chapters 5 and 6. But look at his next statement: "And that is what some of you were. But you were washed, you were sanctified, you were justified in the name of the Lord Jesus Christ and by the Spirit of our God" (v. 11). Despite some highly inappropriate sexual sin within the church, Paul highlights their true identity and urges them to live in accordance with that high calling.

Also, notice Paul's exhortation to the Thessalonians: "Finally, brothers, we instructed you how to live in order to please God, as in fact you are living. Now we ask you and urge you in the Lord Jesus to do this more and more" (1 Thess. 4:1). He sounds this same note in verses 9–10: "Now about brotherly love we do not need to write to you, for you yourselves have been taught by God to love each other. And in fact, you do love all the brothers throughout Macedonia. Yet we urge you, brothers, to do so more and more." Paul basically says, "You're doing a great job! Keep the momentum going."

There is another reason it is important to highlight "redemption in progress" when you counsel someone. When people start to see how God is transforming them in one arena of life, that realization can be "borrowed" or "transferred" to other areas. That is, there is a ripple effect to redemption. When one part of life changes or is in the process of changing, other parts of our lives are more likely to be caught up in the transformation process. This is not simply the power of suggestion. As we witness God's work in one area of our lives, we grow in our belief that he can and will work in other areas. Faith has a momentum. One of the most delightful aspects of counseling is when someone returns to report growth that goes beyond the issues we originally discussed. The gospel is gaining traction in all areas of life.

So, affirm where you see and have seen the Spirit at work. Highlight the places where gospel values characterize your friend's life.

Questions for the Sufferer

Here are several questions to help you understand the person as a sufferer.

1. What significant situational stressors is he currently facing? Consider things like body/health issues ("intrapersonal" influences), relationship pressures ("interpersonal" influences), and circumstantial and social/cultural influences ("extrapersonal" influences).[2]
2. What were the significant shaping events of his life?
3. How has he been sinned against?
4. How is the person experiencing his problems?

The first three questions ask, do you have a clear sense of the different circumstances at play in the person's life? No doubt, the way a person responds to these circumstances reveals whether he is living within a biblical framework or not. Our circumstances do not *determine* in some fatalistic way whether or not we grow in Christ. As I learned during the snowstorm in Maine, the same situation may provoke different responses in different people. Nevertheless, if you don't understand a person's situation, you haven't understood the person, because the person does not live in a vacuum.

The Bible affirms that we impact one another for better or worse. "A gentle answer turns away wrath, but a harsh word stirs up anger" (Prov. 15:1). Fathers *do* exasperate their children (Eph. 6:4). We *can* refresh one another in the Lord (2 Tim. 1:16–18). We create a relational context for other people that makes it easier or harder for them to obey Christ. God recognizes this, and he cares about the suffering that people experience at the hands of others, as we saw in chapter 5.

And for better or for worse, the circumstances of our lives impact us as well. Remember, God's Word always comes tailored to people in specific situations. The things the Corinthians needed to hear were different from what the Galatians needed to hear. The situation in Colosse differed from that in Crete, where Titus was ministering. Paul (and the other biblical writers) didn't write generic documents that were mass-mailed to God's people!

Rather, God used the writers of Scripture to bring timely messages, specifically shaped to the needs and problems of his people. In a similar way, you've got to understand the situational factors at play in a person's life if you hope to bring the Word to her in a specific and helpful way.

The fourth question above reminds us that the entry point into a person's life is usually not her sin but her experience of suffering. Paul Tripp calls counselors to notice the "entry gates" in a person's life as an initial step of personal ministry.[3] The entry gate is not the particular problem that brings the person to you, nor is it the particular circumstances or relationships in the person's life. Rather, the entry gate "is a particular person's *experience* of the situation, problem, or relationship."[4] Entry gate themes might include fear, anger, despair, confusion, shame, or guilt. If you miss the entry gate(s) that people offer as they tell their stories, you will misconnect with them. Launching into an admonition against sin or even highlighting identity in Christ may feel like a "bait and switch" unless people believe that you understand their experiences and are approaching them with empathy and love.

One more thing: it isn't always the difficult things of life that have a negative impact. Good things—blessings—such as a job promotion with a big pay raise can prompt *either* a godly or ungodly response. It's interesting in Philippians 4:10–13 that Paul speaks of being content in "whatever the circumstances," whether "well fed or hungry, whether living in plenty or in want." Ordinarily we think of contentment as elusive in the midst of hardship, but Paul broadens our understanding by noting that, apart from Christ, contentment is elusive whether our circumstances are favorable or unfavorable.

Questions for the Sinner

Here you can ask:

1. What desires, thoughts, emotions, and actions are out of line with gospel/kingdom values?
2. What motives, themes, and interpretations of life "compete" with the biblical story?

These questions help you discover the stories, values, and beliefs that are guiding the person and leading to sinful words, attitudes, emotions, and actions. Recognize that the Bible not only speaks to the more visible aspects of our lives but also to the underlying intentions and attitudes of the heart. Motives are important.

In Luke 6:43–45, Jesus says, "No good tree bears bad fruit, nor does a bad tree bear good fruit. Each tree is recognized by its own fruit. People do not pick figs from thornbushes, or grapes from briers. The good man brings good things out of the good stored up in his heart, and the evil man brings evil things out of the evil stored up in his heart. For out of the overflow of his heart his mouth speaks."

Similarly, in Matthew 15:18–20, Jesus teaches that uncleanness before God is an internal not an external problem: "But the things that come out of the mouth come from the heart, and these make a man 'unclean.' For out of the heart come evil thoughts, murder, adultery, sexual immorality, theft, false testimony, slander. These are what make a man 'unclean.'"

Jesus uses the terminology of "treasure" in Matthew 6:21: "For where your treasure is [i.e., what you have invested with value], there your heart will be also." Our lives are controlled or directed by what we value.[5] We functionally worship what we believe will bring us joy, happiness, peace, contentment, and the like. It's easy to say that we worship God in an ultimate sense, but our daily lives reveal the "functional" gods we serve in the moment.

Here are some additional questions to help you to identify underlying motives and beliefs that reveal the story and values that guide your counselee.[6]

1. What do you want or desire?
2. What do you fear? (i.e., what do you *not* want?)
3. What really matters to you right now?
4. What are you feeling right now?
5. Where (or in what) are you banking your hopes? (What are you hoping will happen?)
6. Complete this sentence, "If only _____, then _____." This question gets at the person's ideal reality.

7. What do you think you need? Why?
8. What can't you live without? (What do you worry about losing?)

The answers to these questions reveal what we *really* think about ourselves, others, and God, moment by moment. They lead to the sinful words and actions that erupt into our relationships.

For example, when I speak to my daughter or son in a harsh tone of voice, it's not enough to say, "I sinned by being harsh." Though that is true, I ought to explore the "whys" behind my words and tone, particularly if there is a pattern. As I reflect on these questions, perhaps I think I need peace and quiet at all costs. Or perhaps I "need" a child who is compliant in order to feel good about my parenting. But these attitudes are antithetical to the gospel! These self-oriented story lines have nothing to do with the self-sacrificial aspects of the kingdom. In the moments leading up to my overt sin, I've been captivated essentially by a story line (really a "story lie") that says, "Your comfort is king. What's wrong here is your child. She's disturbing your peace." Thankfully, the Scriptures speak deeply and redemptively to sinners and invite us to return to gospel-oriented story lines.

As you ask these questions, you should be thinking of alternative values and actions that *are* in line with the gospel. Ask yourself, "What aspects of the good news bring hope, perspective, and direction to this person's struggles?" Already the wheels should be turning in terms of what Scripture passages and themes may function in those ways.

To sum up, realize that when you minister to people who are simultaneously saints, sufferers, and sinners, you will often need to prioritize. You may judge that the need of the hour is comfort in their distress (even though you see places where they are responding to circumstances in an ungodly way). Or you sense that addressing their sin is a priority, even though their sin occurs in the context of another person's sin against them. In this way, to review from chapter 5, we use the Bible in multifaceted ways: (1) The Bible *confirms* the identity of the saint; (2) The Bible *comforts* the sufferer;

and (3) The Bible *confronts* the sinner. Confirmation, comfort, and confrontation—all have a place in personal ministry, and the Scriptures function in all three modes.

Let's turn now to questions that can help you wisely read a given passage.

Questions to Help You Understand the Passage

These questions will help you to do three things: (1) understand a passage in its original context, (2) understand a passage in the larger context of redemptive history, and (3) move toward application. Once again, remember that answering these questions exhaustively is not required for a life-changing encounter with God through his Word! Nor is transformation into the character of Christ guaranteed as a result of detailed study. We are dependent on God's Spirit for insight and life change, whether we look at a passage for five minutes or fifty-five (or longer)! But when we are able to dig deeper in our personal study of Scripture or in preparation for an appointment with someone, we will stand even more amazed at the depth and relevance of God's Word.

Original Context

This step involves wrestling with the way a text may have been understood by its original recipients. This includes the need for careful study of the historical, grammatical, and literary features of the text, as well as how a particular passage fits into the rest of the book. Many available books on biblical interpretation can help in this regard.[7] I would encourage you to read at least one of them in conjunction with this book. But don't be intimidated by this task if you have not received formal training in studying Scripture. Realize that with Spirit-led, careful observation, a good study Bible, and the insights of other believers, you don't necessarily need a library full of other resources.[8] So, what questions can you ask that will help to flesh out the original context? Here are some suggestions.

1. What has happened in redemptive history up to the time the passage/book was written? You want to know where you are in the story. This is done even in the entertainment industry. TV shows with a continuing story line often begin a new show with "Previously on. . . ." So before launching into the study of a passage, it is important to have a basic idea of what happened "previously in redemptive history."

2. Based upon careful study of the historical, grammatical, and literary features of the passage, what do you think God and the human author were trying to communicate to their audience at this particular point in redemptive history? How does this connect with the emphases for the book as a whole? Where do you see the theme(s) of your passage elsewhere in the book? These last two questions suggest the importance of understanding a passage within its larger context. Even if you have not recently read the biblical book in which your passage is situated, reading the introduction to the book in your study Bible orients you to the main emphases and themes.

3. Here's another way of putting it: What pastoral-theological aim(s) does the author have in writing this portion of Scripture? What seems to be the main theme/point, keeping in mind the thematic or theological aims for the book as a whole? It may be helpful to summarize the passage with a short sentence.

4. What response do you think the author intended? That is, how might this passage have affected the lives of the original audience? How do you think they might have ideally responded to God's message to them?

These questions prime you for application. How a passage of Scripture might have been understood and lived out *then* at least suggests some ways it may be used today.[9]

Larger Context of Redemptive History

The next step is to understand how the passage and its message fit in God's larger story. Here are questions and comments that will help you.

1. Why do you think this passage was particularly important at the stage of redemptive history in which it was written? In other words, how do you think this passage contributes to God's unfolding revelation? How would the story line of the Bible be different if this passage or book were not included?

2. How is the main theme, thought, or emphasis of your passage developed in later writings? Similarly, in what earlier portions of the Bible do you find this theme, even if not fully developed? How has your passage advanced an earlier understanding of the main theme/thought? This is the reading "backward and forward" mentioned earlier. Here is where using cross-references, concordances, and study Bible notes can be helpful. Of course, they are not infallible, nor should they limit the scriptural connections you might make.

3. How is your passage an "unfinished story"? What questions or unresolved tensions remain at its end? This will be particularly evident in Old Testament passages, but remember that redemptive history doesn't end until Jesus returns to consummate his kingdom. Therefore, New Testament passages have this forward-looking thrust as well.

4. How do the themes of your passage connect with the life, death, and resurrection of Jesus Christ? For Old Testament passages you could ask, how does the coming of Jesus (the gospel) complete (or give an unexpected twist to) your passage's story line? For a Gospel account you might ask, how does the writer portray the in-breaking of God's kingdom in Christ? What aspects of the kingdom's coming does he highlight? What do we learn about Jesus himself? For a New Testament passage you might ask, how does the climax of redemption in Jesus anchor this story or teaching?

5. More specifically, what connections are there with the church, the body of Christ and possessor of his Spirit? Remember, although the coming of Jesus—his life, death, and resurrection—is the climax of the biblical story, the story of the gospel continues to work itself out in the life of the church.[10]

To make these kinds of intrabiblical connections, there is no substitute for a growing breadth and depth knowledge of Scripture. If we (and I'm including myself!) are not growing in biblical literacy, our use of Scripture will tend to become more narrow, limited, and superficial. People we serve will sense that, rather than getting a Thanksgiving feast, they are getting leftover turkey tetrazzini a week later! May God give us insight to see the many connecting points between passages so that we and others would say, along with Paul, "Oh, the depth of the riches of the wisdom and knowledge of God!" (Rom. 11:33).

Moving toward Application

Now you are better equipped to consider how the passage might be used in a particular ministry situation. Here are potentially helpful questions.

1. How does this passage, in light of the gospel connections just made, address God's people as saints, sufferers, and sinners? Notice that we shouldn't try to force an answer to each question. The passage may well be weighted toward only one of the three. But it's worth asking:
   a. What does this passage say about the identity and privilege of being part of God's people?
   b. What does it say about the nature and purpose of suffering and how God approaches the sufferer?
   c. What does the passage say or suggest about the conduct of God's people, in view of their identity? In other words, how does the message of the passage shape your thoughts, attitudes, emotions, or actions? What does it look like to turn to God now in light of

this passage? Notice that passages will not give you the exact shape of gospel obedience! You are always adapting the thrust of a passage for your specific time, place, and person, seeking to live in greater love for God and neighbor.

2. A more generic or open-ended question might be, how does this passage give your person a better "lens" to interpret his experiences? In view of that, how should he live before God and others?

Remember that application is not simply a cognitive exercise, a kind of "thought replacement" task in which we substitute good and true thoughts for false thoughts and idolatrous motives. True application—living wisely in light of the passage—is always a relational experience that involves our whole being. Fruitful application warms our hearts toward God and others. It realigns our thoughts and attitudes according to the contours of God's truth. It involves concrete actions that evidence outwardly our devotion to God and service to others. Wise application is nothing less than wholehearted worship of God and tangible love for others.[11]

Why Make It So Complicated?!

Even after my opening remarks to this chapter, you may be asking why I'm making it so complicated. Why not just ask, "What principle in this passage might help this person?" That may not be a completely illegitimate question (as I discussed earlier in chapter 2), but do you remember what happens when we divide up the Bible into smaller bits? We may not actually challenge the lies and idolatries we live by. Bits of Bible may not have bite in our lives and the lives of those we hope to help.

There may be many reasons a person doesn't grab hold of the truth or an encounter with God's Word doesn't bring change. But one reason may be because we have failed to help that person locate the passage *and* her life within the grand drama of God. Unless she sees how a passage invites her to live within God's great redemptive drama, the conclusion "This passage is irrelevant to my life" is a potential response.

As philosopher Alasdair MacIntyre says, "I can only answer the question, 'What am I to do?' [and I would add, Why should I do it?] if I can answer the prior question, 'Of what story or stories do I find myself a part?'"[12]

I hope that the questions in this chapter will equip you to understand and to connect the stories of people's lives with the story of Scripture. Although I am proposing a certain methodology, I want to stress that this framework should serve as a guide, not as a "recipe book" for personal ministry. Ultimately, if we are privileged to be part of someone's growth in Christ, it is because God the Holy Spirit has been pleased to bring that to fruition (1 Cor. 3:7). By all means, use these tools, but use them in humble reliance on the Holy Spirit and in community with other discerning believers.

Discussion Questions

1. What has been your methodology to connect people with Scripture? How do the last two chapters impact your approach to people and to Scripture?
2. What barriers do you anticipate in employing this model in your own life and ministry?
3. Consider someone you are ministering to and use the "Questions to Help You Understand the Person" to further your understanding of this person. Was the approach helpful? Why or why not?
4. Consider a passage of Scripture you have recently read. Use the "Questions to Help You Understand the Passage" to explore the passage. Were the questions helpful? Why or why not?

CHAPTER 8

Introducing Tom
and Natalie

In the next three chapters, I would like to get specific about the model I've described and show you how to use it with a particular passage and ministry situation. Actually, I want to apply one Old Testament passage and one New Testament passage to two people with very different struggles and questions. This will illustrate how a single passage can connect with multiple life situations. It will also demonstrate how two (or more!) quite different passages of Scripture can be used with a single person in the midst of specific struggles and concerns.

What I will do in these chapters looks like this:

	Reading the Person	Connecting with the Old Testament	Connecting with the New Testament
Tom	Chapter 8	Chapter 9	Chapter 10
Natalie	Chapter 8	Chapter 9	Chapter 10

Let's begin by hearing about Tom.[1]

Tom's Story

Tom is a thirty-two-year-old man, married for twelve years, and the father of three children. He comes to you to discuss his marriage. He is concerned that his wife Sarah may leave him after learning of his recently renewed struggle with Internet pornography.

Tom reports that his exposure to pornographic materials began in his preteen years while living with his mother and stepfather. His parents were divorced when he was three years old, and he has had only occasional contact with his biological father. He is an only child. His stepfather, who was much older than his mother, had a cache of magazines and pornographic novellas that Tom would frequently read. He was not a Christian at the time, nor were any other family members. During high school he was sexually active and had multiple partners. He recalls fending for himself most days as his mother and stepfather worked long hours.

During his freshman year in college, Tom had a Christian roommate and came to Christ through his witness. Immediately his sexual behaviors—fornication, masturbation, and viewing pornography—ceased, and he began to grow in the Lord. He did struggle at times with guilt and regret over the years he had pursued his lusts, but he found increasing rest in the forgiveness of Jesus.

In his sophomore year he met Sarah, who had transferred to his college and joined their campus fellowship. They began to date and soon were sexually involved. Although they confided their struggle to their campus ministry leader, their sexual activity continued and Sarah became pregnant. They got married in Tom's junior year but both dropped out of school so Tom could work full time and Sarah could care for the baby.

They had a difficult first year of marriage. Both of them struggled with regret and with anger toward the other. Tom felt guilty, ashamed, and responsible for their predicament. He struggled with feeling like a failure as a Christian and as a husband. They received counseling for approximately four months, and both felt that real progress occurred in their relationship.

Tom's struggle with pornography resurfaced about three years into their marriage. Although he had occasionally viewed porn on the Internet prior to that time, he began to look at it regularly. He said, "I knew it was wrong, but I wanted some escape from the pressures of a new job. Sarah was absolutely exhausted caring for two young children, and I felt I couldn't burden her with my struggles at work. I think we both felt pretty alone. I retreated into a world that gave me some sense of power, control, and pleasure that I didn't have at work or on the home front."

Sarah was devastated when she found Tom's stash of porn magazines and DVDs, which he had used after she was asleep for the night. He sought counseling for approximately six months through his church. Sarah also sought help in her struggle to forgive Tom. They both would say that God brought healing into their relationship at that time.

In the years that followed, Tom struggled intermittently with Internet pornography. He was most likely to struggle when work or financial pressures were great or when he and Sarah were having conflicts. The most sustained struggle occurred about two years ago when, for several weeks, he visited pornographic Web sites late at night for several hours at a time. Sarah was suspicious of his delayed bedtimes and somewhat detached demeanor. She checked the computer record of the sites he had visited and confronted him. At that time she said that if she ever found him doing this again, she would consider a divorce for sexual infidelity. Tom got into an accountability and discipling relationship at church, and both his struggle and the tenor of their marriage improved. However, Tom believes that the warmth they had experienced in the earlier years of their marriage was not really present to a great extent. He believes Sarah has kept him at a distance to protect herself. Occasionally, Sarah would question him about his use of pornography. They did not receive marriage counseling on this occasion—Sarah viewed the problem as Tom's.

Tom admits that over time he became lax in accountability relationships and drifted into a "maintenance mode" with Sarah. They had less times of substantial conversation, less physical intimacy, and no real sharing of their spiritual lives. He said, "Sometimes it felt more like we were roommates and coparents than husband and wife." He admits, "I wasn't even sure how to connect more deeply. I felt a lot of inadequacy. Who was I to be the leader in our family? I don't think Sarah has ever really respected me, and I don't blame her."

More frequently he daydreamed about what life could have been like if he and Sarah had remained pure and he had finished college. He had always anticipated several years of a "fun" marriage before facing the rigors of family life. He had also anticipated graduating with a degree in architecture, but he continues to work outside that field as a sales manager for a midsized company that manufactures garden tools.

About two months ago, after missing out on a promotion at work, feeling the weight of increasing debt, and experiencing a growing sense of discontent and inadequacy, Tom began to visit pornographic Web sites again. Yet he felt convicted and stopped of his own accord after a few days. "I knew this was sin against God and against Sarah, and I didn't want to go down that dead-end road again." He wrestled with whether to tell Sarah, given her ultimatum two years earlier. In the end he decided that "living in the shadows was not an option." He had hoped that his honesty would count for something.

Sarah's response was initially one of anger, then grim resignation. She has said, "I knew I couldn't trust you!" "I was right to keep waiting for the other shoe to drop." "From the start you have been unfaithful to me and to the Lord." She has talked of separation but taken no action. She is not interested in pursuing marriage counseling—"I'm not sure Tom can do anything that will make a difference." Several men at church, including one of the elders, regularly meet with Tom, but they have suggested that he begin talking with you as well. Two mature women in the church have started to meet with Sarah.

Here are some of the things Tom said when you met with him: "This time I've blown it for good." "It can never be like it was supposed to be." "There's no way to repair the damage I've caused." "What does this mean for our children?" "Have I derailed God's plan for my life? Maybe I did that way back when I got Sarah pregnant." "I want to believe that God is for us, but I'm not so sure I haven't ruined his plan and exhausted his patience.

I don't have a lot of hope that he's up to something good here."
"I've felt a lot more temptation regarding the Internet since every-thing blew up. So far, so good, but sometimes I think, what's the point of obedience that's too little, too late?"

"Reading" (Interpreting) Tom's Story

If you were actually counseling Tom, you would ask him many more questions. It is likely that you would (and should!) be much more tentative in your interpretation of his struggle. But for the sake of illustrating the connection between life and Scripture, I'm going to mention a few initial thoughts using the three biblical categories of saint, sufferer, and sinner and the associated questions from the last chapter. Before you proceed, ask yourself, "How do I understand Tom? What are the dominant themes or story lines in his life? What does he need most right now?"

Saint: Where Are the Marks of Grace in His Life? Where Is He Living True to His Identity as a Son of the Living God?

These are the places of growth that remind Tom that the dominant plotlines of his life don't fall exclusively into negative categories.

Tom's pattern has been to hide his sin until Sarah discovers it. This time he seemed to have a real sense of his sin before God and Sarah on his own. He chose to come into the light. Repentance, not mere regret, seems to characterize his response, and that is in line with the gospel. Tom may regret telling Sarah, given the fallout in their relationship, but his desire to live honestly and openly before God and his wife is a sign of dependence on God.

He's part of a community of faith and welcomes the involvement of other Christians in this struggle. This is like money in the bank! Too often, those caught in a pattern of sin isolate themselves. This means he has others, besides yourself, who are speaking into his struggle.

Last, he's struggling with sinful desires, but he is still honestly wrestling before God. He seems to have a soft heart. Doubt more

111

than defiance seems to be his posture, and that realization will shape the way you approach him.

Sufferer: What Circumstances Impact His Struggle?

Certainly Tom's distant past plays a role; namely, his parents' divorce, his early exposure to pornography, and his lack of parental oversight. How he thinks about those shaping influences is important. He grew up essentially fatherless, and we might wonder how such a relational "hole" continues to impact his view of himself, of other relationships, and of God. We know he feels inadequate as a husband. Does his sense of inadequacy and failure run more deeply because he was so often left to himself? Does he feel that God is a distant and uninvolved parent?

More recently, his financial struggles and job disappointments seem to be linked to his recent upsurge in sexual struggle. Another way to assess the impact of present circumstances is to ask, "What triggers tempt Tom to sin in this way?" We also know that relational conflict is a breeding ground for his struggle—and the conflict is higher than perhaps it's ever been. Of course, Scripture never puts the blame on someone else for our sin, but knowing the relational pressures and challenges a person faces fleshes out the ministry approach beyond mere rebuke for sin.

From the information presented, we have a sense that daily life in his marriage has been a fairly lonely place for Tom (and Sarah). No doubt, he has contributed to that distance, but neither of them seems very proactive in the relationship. Tom does not know how to bridge the distance between them, and his recent sin has only widened that gap. Since his confession of sin, nothing Sarah has communicated gives him hope for their marriage. In fact, she has been quite pessimistic in her attitude toward him and their marriage. If Sarah's assessment—"unfaithful, untrustworthy, hopeless"—remains the only lens through which Tom views himself and the marriage, it is no wonder that he has little hope or motivation for further change.

He is acutely aware that he is suffering the consequences of his sin. He wonders if he has irreversibly changed the course of his life and the lives of Sarah and his children. He is weighed down under that burden.

Sinner: What Desires, Thoughts, Emotions, and Actions Are Out of Line with Kingdom Values and Therefore "Compete" with the Biblical Story?

What does Tom want? Historically, rather than engage with Sarah (or God) in the midst of life challenges, Tom has chosen to escape into pornography. It is a place of safety and refuge for him. "Interacting" with fantasy women is less intimidating than confronting real problems or dealing with real relationships in a constructive way. Perhaps pornography is a place of control and mastery for him, which for a short time whispers, "You are not inadequate."

It doesn't seem that Tom consistently brings his failures and disappointments to God. In many ways, he is living like an orphan. He chafes at his place in life but has resisted facing these realities with a distinctively biblical worldview or with confidence in the power of God. You also get the sense that he's a bit angry that he did the right thing (confess his sin) but God allowed it to blow up.

His dominant struggle right now seems to be one of genuine fear for the future, as well as an element of self-pity. (That's the "why bother?" attitude.) He's discouraged but that discouragement could potentially lead to him giving up and diving headlong into sexual sin. There also seem to be elements of guilt and regret from his statements, "I've blown it for good" and "derailed God's plans."

What's Next?

With this understanding of Tom's story, what is most needed right now to help Tom live in light of the gospel? What does he need to see of our triune God's character and work that would shape the way he's looking at his life? What gospel-motivated changes ought to occur so that he is more consistently living in the biblical plotline? What is your task as a counselor or mentor? Is it to help him consider various practical ways he can live sacrificially as Sarah's husband? Is it to affirm his identity as a beloved child of God? Is it to challenge him for his lack of faith? It could be any or all of these things! But what is most pressing? I think it is to encourage him to press forward in hope and to assure him that God's redemptive purposes for his (and Sarah's) lives continue. No doubt, ongoing ministry to him will need to include other aspects of his struggle, but I think this would be a helpful place to start. Early in the counseling process, many people simply need hope. They need to see a God who has not abandoned them to their own devices and who meets them with grace and mercy in their time of need.

So, if you were going to use a specific portion of Scripture to minister to Tom, what passage would you choose to bring hope and assurance of God's ongoing redemptive work in his life? I would imagine if I polled individual readers of this book, each one would suggest different, potentially helpful passages. And that's the beauty of using Scripture in ministry! There is no "right" passage you must use. In the next chapter, we'll pick up Tom's story, connecting him with God's story as given in an Old Testament passage. Now, let's hear about Natalie.

Natalie's Story

Natalie is a forty-two-year-old single pediatrician who comes to you seeking advice for issues related to her work. She is a strong believer, having professed Christ at a young age. She comes from an intact family and has two brothers and a sister ranging in age from twenty-six to thirty-five. Two of her siblings (one brother and the sister) are involved in full-time Christian ministry.

Natalie recalls a nurturing, godly home environment in which her parents encouraged each child's gifts and interests. Natalie's wide-ranging interests included academics, sports (tennis and swimming), music (piano), and art (drawing and watercolors). She was actively involved as a leader in her youth group during high school. She was a straight-A student (valedictorian) and varsity athlete. She admits, "I was fairly driven, but it was all internal. I didn't feel any pressure from my parents. I *was* conscious of wanting to be a model for my younger siblings. I guess you could say that I had perfectionist tendencies."

During her collegiate years Natalie was actively involved in an urban Lutheran church that had several ministries to the poor and underserved in the neighborhood. She saw firsthand the deleterious effects of poverty on the health of children and prayerfully decided to pursue medical training. Following a pediatric residency in another city, she joined a small multi-specialty clinic in one of the most poverty-stricken areas of the city.

The work was grueling. Seventy- to eighty-hour weeks were the norm early on as she did both inpatient and outpatient care. "Those years were tough. I was tired most of the time, but I remember how the Lord sustained me each day. I also remember many conversations with my coworkers about how my faith in Christ made a difference in the way I approached my workday." Over the last six years the pace has improved somewhat as more physicians joined the group.

Still, she has found it difficult to be very involved in her home church because of the ongoing time commitments at work. "I do have two close female friends at church, although one of them is getting married, so I expect the dynamic of the relationship to change." Natalie had a serious dating relationship in her mid-thirties, but the relationship ended when Natalie decided not to relocate to be near her boyfriend when he secured a teaching position in a small college. "It was the hardest decision of my life. I deeply cared for Jerry, but I really sensed that the Lord's calling was for me to stay here. At least back then, it felt a little too comfortable to move to a place with white picket fences!"

Over the past two years she has experienced a growing struggle with what she sees as the relative lack of impact of her work. "I'm not sure what difference I'm really making in the grand scheme of things. No doubt my relationships with these single moms have resulted in better overall health for their children as they are growing. But I've seen many of these children grow older and move right into the same cycle of teenage motherhood, drug use, or worse. Although I have shared the love of Christ in deed, and not infrequently in word, I've seen very few come to

Christ. And those who have made professions of faith have had very little fruit in their lives. No one seems to escape the inertia of urban poverty. My efforts so often seem futile.

"Day after day I get caught up in quick, problem-oriented visits—a sore throat, a well-baby check, the flu, constipation—and I wonder, *Am I missing something here?* When did my work move from joy to toil? I've been asking myself lately, would I do more good as a youth worker on staff at a church? Would that potentially provide an opportunity for greater spiritual impact? For deeper relationships? I see both in my brother's and sister's ministries. Sure, they have their fair share of struggle and there's a 'toil' aspect to their work at times as well. But overall, they seem to be both passionate and content about what they do. I feel like I've lost passion and contentment over the last two or three years. Some days I dread going to work. It never used to be like that. It's been hard to find joy in the Lord and in what I'm doing."

Although Natalie has sacrificed financially and relationally to minister at the health center, she says, "If I had it to do over again, I think I would. I really have sensed God's guidance throughout and have always felt that he wanted me to persevere in this work. But now, I'm much less sure." Natalie's friends at church have been very supportive although several are urging her to consider options other than remaining at the health center. "They tell me to consider whether what I'm experiencing might be 'holy discontent,' a growing sense that the Lord might be moving me in a different direction. But the thought of doing something else still feels like a betrayal of the people and the mission for whom I have labored for so long."

Interpreting Natalie's Story

As with Tom, many other details of Natalie's life would shape the specific ways in which the gospel speaks to her, but let's begin with what we know now. Using the same three "identity categories" of saint, sufferer, and sinner, what themes from Natalie's story seem important?

Saint: Where Are the Marks of Grace in Her Life? Where Is She Living True to Her Identity as a Daughter of the Living God?

I think this aspect of Natalie's identity sounds the clearest note. Have you ever felt like you were standing on holy ground when you spoke with someone? Have you ever felt challenged and ministered to just by hearing someone's struggle and the ways in which she has sought to follow Jesus in the midst of it? That's how I felt hearing Natalie's story. What strikes me most are not the ways in which she *fails* to live by God's story but the many ways in which she has sought to live for her King. Such a perspective suggests that much of your ministry to her, at least initially, will be one of encouragement, not simply advice-giving or vocational counseling.

I want to affirm Natalie's choices to minister to the poor and the marginalized so dear to God's heart. I want to celebrate the fact that she has not bought into the elusive dreams of wealth, and the safety and comfort so many believe come with riches. I want to commend her perseverance in a taxing ministry. I want to remember, with her, God's faithfulness to her and her colleagues.

Such reminders of God's works of grace in her life are part of a perspective-setting ministry agenda for her life. Too often we get discouraged in our labors because we forget the bigger story we are a part of. In times of transition in the Old Testament, God repeatedly reminds his people of his faithful works in bringing them to the present (Gen. 17; Deut. 1—11; Josh. 24; Pss. 105—106). So it's entirely appropriate to place Natalie's current struggles in the broader context of God's clear work in her life.

Sufferer: What Circumstances Impact Her Struggle?

It is clear that Natalie experiences the brokenness of the world around her. Her doubts and her wrestling are provoked by the challenges of inner-city medical ministry. She lives in an environment where hope so easily evaporates. Where systemic problems constantly undermine her best efforts. Where her sacrifices seem fruitless. No doubt she has seen God's hand in her life and work, but lately the cumulative weight of suffering around her has dimmed her vision of God's advancing kingdom.

If you fail to take seriously the very difficult setting in which Natalie works, your approach to her will be superficial, not "real life." It will feel like a spiritualized version of "Don't Worry, Be Happy." Scripture never minimizes the challenges God's people face, nor should we.

One area to explore further is the issue of relationships. Natalie said several things that make me wonder what it's like for her to be a single professional woman in her early forties. Would she like to be married? Does she wonder about her decision to end the relationship with Jerry? How is she experiencing the relational costs of her vocational commitments? Compared to her high-school and collegiate years, her life is ultrafocused on her medical practice. How do these real costs potentially fuel discouragement about her lack of impact?

Sinner: What Desires, Thoughts, Emotions, and Actions Are Out of Line with Kingdom Values and Therefore "Compete" with the Biblical Story?

As I noted above, what strikes me most about Natalie are the ways she *is* living in line with the story of the kingdom. Unlike Tom, who clearly was making choices contrary to kingdom values, Natalie appears to be "weary in *well doing*" (Gal. 6:9, KJV).

That is not to say that Natalie has handled her challenges perfectly. As you get to know her, you may find deeper taproots to her discouragement, including high standards for what "success" in medical ministry looks like. She has a history of high achievement and impact in others' lives. Has she finally met her match? Perhaps her admitted perfectionism has developed into a propensity to highlight the negative and overlook the positive. Is too much of her identity tied up in being "Pediatrician for the Underserved"? Does her perceived lack of long-term impact undermine her identity and sense of worth?

Certainly, if some of these hypotheses prove true, she needs biblical reorientation or correction. But addressing potential sin issues would not be the first note I sound in ministry to Natalie. Doing so would ignore the more prominent features of her life story. Further, it's not always true that people need correction for *willful* sin. They may simply need God's ways explained more adequately to them. That may be the case with Natalie. She may simply need to get a fuller, richer picture of what kingdom impact "looks like" to build her faith. In ministry, we want to differentiate between ignorance, unintentional sin, and intentional sin.

What's Next?

Natalie should strike us as a godly woman who has become weary and disheartened in the midst of intense medical ministry. She is having a hard time seeing kingdom impact to her work, and she wonders if she should pursue serving God in another vocation. Her "entry gate" is discouragement, and I want my use of Scripture to bring her encouragement and hope in the midst of her battle fatigue. In the next chapter we will see how a particular Old Testament passage offers such encouragement to her.

Discussion Questions

1. Consider Tom and Natalie. Was the saint/sufferer/sinner distinction helpful to you in organizing their stories? Why or why not? Is there anything you would add to any of the three areas?
2. What biblical perspective or truth do you think Tom most needs to hear right now? What about Natalie?
3. Brainstorm two or three passages (Old Testament and New Testament) that you might use with Tom. Why did you pick those passages?
4. Brainstorm several passages that you might use with Natalie. Why did you pick them?

CHAPTER 9

Tom, Natalie, and the Old Testament

At the end of the previous chapter I asked you to consider what Old Testament passage(s) you might use with Tom and Natalie. My guess is that you traveled in a life-to-text direction, considering the themes of Tom and Natalie's lives and thinking of passages that had significant thematic overlap. It's likely that I would hear your choices and say, "Yes, I can see how that passage would connect." But you may not initially say the same about my choice!

I have decided to use Haggai 2:1–9. You may think, *That's as challenging as the genealogies of 1 Chronicles!* Well, not quite! It *is* true that Haggai has a canyon feel to it on first glance. After all, how often do we use the Minor Prophets in personal ministry?

But there is a method to my madness! My choice of Haggai doesn't come out of the blue. God used this passage to encourage me long ago at a time when I wondered if my sin was going to irreversibly alter my life. Although the details of my experiences are different from Tom's, I can identify with his sense of futility and hopelessness and I believe Haggai speaks to that. Second, I have prepared a sermon on this passage and used it as a passage for discussion in my Biblical Interpretation class. Finally, I chose this passage because I wanted a passage that didn't have a tried-and-true feel to it. I want to demonstrate that we *can* go to less familiar places in Scripture to find wisdom for today. I want to

121

show you the untapped potential of many Bible passages to help people with the problems they are facing.

Let me comment further about passage selection. Rather than minister using a passage of my choice, sometimes I will ask the people I counsel what passages have been most meaningful to *them* lately. That becomes a good starting place because they already have a connection to God's Word that can be deepened with more discussion. Remember that the more unfamiliar a person is with the Bible, the more important it is to choose a passage with a more obvious connection to the person's struggle. If you have to work too hard to help someone see what *you* see, perhaps someplace else in Scripture is more appropriate. (Or maybe you need to revisit *your* understanding of the chosen text!) But remember, you're not usually conducting an inductive Bible study in one-on-one ministry, especially in a more formal counseling situation.

Lastly, I'm not expecting you to meet Tom or Natalie, brainstorm, and then pick Haggai out of thin air, studying for hours in preparation for your next meeting. Nor do I expect you to keep Tom or Natalie in the hallway while you frantically put a passage through its paces (using the questions I outlined earlier) in order to discuss it with them! I chose Haggai because I have a *cumulative familiarity* with it and I see some thematic overlap with Tom or Natalie. No doubt you have such passages in your life too. In short, my previous personal familiarity, application, and study prepared me to use Haggai in ministry to Tom and Natalie. I trust that you are primed to use other passages because of *your* previous study and meditation on Scripture. Hopefully we are all growing in our abilities to use the Scriptures *widely* and *deeply*.

Reading (Interpreting) Haggai 2:1–9

As I did in interpreting Tom and Natalie's stories, I will use the questions proposed in chapter 7 to guide our understanding of Haggai. I encourage you to take a quick read through the book of Haggai to better understand what I'll say below. Or take a look at the introduction to Haggai in your study Bible. Feel free to answer the questions yourself before reading my thoughts. Take a look at Haggai 2:1–9:

On the twenty-first day of the seventh month, the word of the LORD came through the prophet Haggai: "Speak to Zerubbabel son of Shealtiel, governor of Judah, to Joshua son of Jehozadak, the high priest, and to the remnant of the people. Ask them, 'Who of you is left who saw this house in its former glory? How does it look to you now? Does it not seem to you like nothing? But now be strong, O Zerubbabel,' declares the LORD. 'Be strong, O Joshua son of Jehozadak, the high priest. Be strong, all you people of the land,' declares the LORD, 'and work. For I am with you,' declares the LORD Almighty. 'This is what I covenanted with you when you came out of Egypt. And my Spirit remains among you. Do not fear.' This is what the LORD Almighty says: 'In a little while I will once more shake the heavens and the earth, the sea and the dry land. I will shake all nations, and the desired of all nations will come, and I will fill this house with glory,' says the LORD Almighty.[1] 'The silver is mine and the gold is mine,' declares the LORD Almighty. 'The glory of this present house will be greater than the glory of the former house,' says the LORD Almighty. 'And in this place I will grant peace,' declares the LORD Almighty."

Original Context

Let's begin by thinking about the development of redemptive history at the time Haggai was written. So, what has preceded Haggai's prophecy in redemptive history? God has redeemed the descendants of Abraham and formed them into the nation of Israel (Exodus). After a period of rule by various judges (Judges), the monarchy is established, which reaches its high point in the reigns of David and Solomon (1 and 2 Samuel; 1 Kings 1—11; 1 Chronicles; 2 Chron. 1—9). But it's mostly been downhill since that time (1 Kings 12—22; 2 Kings; 2 Chron. 10—36).

After Solomon dies, the kingdom of Israel splits into two: Israel and Judah. Israel, governed by one bad king after another, is conquered by the Assyrians in 722 BC. Judah, governed by both good kings and bad, eventually falls to the Babylonians in 586 BC. At that point the Babylonians destroy the glorious temple that David envisioned and Solomon built—the dwelling place of God—and deport the people to Babylon.

But the Lord has promised a return from exile and, accordingly, in 538 BC, Cyrus, king of Persia (Persia had conquered Babylon in the meantime), decrees that the exiles should return to Jerusalem in Judah in order to rebuild the temple (Ezra 1:1–4). The people return and rebuild the altar and the foundation of the temple (Ezra 3), but they abandon the project due to opposition (Ezra 4).

That brings us to the "present" (at least to 520 BC!). In Haggai 1 we find that the people, spurred on by Haggai's prophecy, resume building the temple. Approximately one month later, the prophecy recorded in 2:1–9 occurs.[2] (You can find all the details of the last two paragraphs in a good study Bible introduction to Haggai, or by using cross-references.)[3] With this history in mind we now can dive into the passage at hand.

The next step is to address the question, What do you think God was trying to communicate to his people at this particular point in redemptive history? That is, based on a close reading (awareness of historical, grammatical, and literary features of the text), what would you judge to be the main theme or point?

Clearly, it has something to do with "temple" (and this is in keeping with the entire book's temple focus). More specifically, it seems like the first three verses are highlighting the people's discouragement in the midst of rebuilding. God voices what they are thinking, particularly those who were old enough to remember the glory of Solomon's temple. (Your cross-references direct you to Ezra 3:12, which supports this view.) "Does it [the new temple] seem to you like nothing?" The problem was that the new temple appeared to be glory deficient! How would God address this concern?

In verses 4–5 God assures the people of his presence, that what he promised them so long ago when he redeemed them from Egypt was still true to this day. Despite their many failures— even their giving up on building the temple since their return— he assured them that his Spirit remained among them. This is a promise for the present that is meant to strengthen their labors.

Then God gives them a series of promises for the future, starting in verse 6 and culminating with verse 9: "'The glory of this present house will be greater than the glory of the former house,' says the LORD Almighty. 'And in this place I will grant peace,' declares the LORD Almighty."[4] At some point, the future glory of the present temple would eclipse the former glory of Solomon's temple.

I could summarize the passage like this: "Present sorrow and fear are overturned by the promise of God's presence and the promise of a greater display of his glory in the temple." This is not the only way to capture the thrust of the passage, but the main theme or message of this passage is NOT:

- If at first you don't succeed, try, try again.
- Quit whining and get to work because God is with you.
- Do the right thing and God will bless you and reverse the consequences of your sin. (This becomes even clearer as we look at where history goes after this prophecy.)

In light of this theme, we need to ask, What response do you think the author intended? That is, how might this passage have affected the lives of the original audience? Ask yourself, "As a Jew living at this time, if I truly grasped the significance of this passage, I would _____." Likely, the intended response was a renewed dedication and hope in the midst of rebuilding efforts. God specifically calls them to "be strong" and "work" and "do not fear." In essence God says, "I know this temple looks like a shack compared to Solomon's temple, but trust that I am with you and that one day greater glory will fill this temple."

Expanded (Redemptive-Historical) Context

The next step is to consider Haggai 2:1–9 in the larger context of Scripture as a whole, beginning with the question, Why was this passage particularly important at this time in redemptive history? In other words, how does this passage contribute to God's unfolding revelation?

The temple was the center of Jewish religious, social, and political life. No temple meant no dwelling place for God. No temple meant no sacrifices, which meant no atonement for sin.

125

In our fragmented, mobile society, it's difficult to imagine a place that would carry so much significance. But the rebuilding of the temple was essential to reaffirm the identity, worship, and life of the Jews as God's people.

Now let's ask specifically, How is the main theme/thought from your passage present in earlier and later writings? We also ask, How does this theme connect with Jesus Christ and his church? Remember, I focused on the temple theme as well as the idea of greater glory. Here you might check out cross-references. You might also look up the word *temple* or *glory* in a concordance (or in a Bible software program) to view potentially relevant connections. If you had more time, you might explore related concepts, including tabernacle, presence of God, house of God, and Tent of Meeting. I have found a helpful resource for tracing themes throughout Scripture in Ryken, Wilhoit, and Longman's *Dictionary of Biblical Imagery*.[5] Of course, there is no substitute for thoughtfully reading the Bible cover to cover, year to year, carefully considering the relationships between different books and passages, including connections with the climax of redemption in Jesus Christ.

As you continue to read, you may ask, "How much of this redemptive-historical study is enough?" If you have a relatively short amount of study time, simply ask the question, "In what ways does this passage connect with Jesus and his renewing rule?" This will push you in a gospel-centered direction as you consider the significance of the passage for today. If you have more time, you will find treasures galore as you ponder the interconnections between the various books and time periods of the Bible. So, let me take the time to open the treasure chest and show you how this might look with Haggai.

From Genesis onward, it has always been God's design to dwell among his people. Following humanity's fall into sin, Genesis 3:8 notes, "Then the man and his wife heard the sound of the LORD God as he was walking in the garden in the cool of the day, and they hid from the LORD God among the trees of the garden." One of sin's first results was that God's own image bearers ran from his presence. But God's rescue plan included a new people descended from Abraham (the people of Israel) redeemed from slavery in Egypt and a new Eden (the Promised

Land). God would not abandon his people. During the exodus God manifested his presence in the pillar of fire or cloud; he traveled *with* his people. Nearly half the book of Exodus concerns the instructions for and the building of the tabernacle so that God could dwell among them (Exod. 25:8). As Moses says in Exodus 33:12–17, God's presence is what distinguishes the Israelites from all the other nations.

Following the entry into the Promised Land and the establishment of the monarchy, Solomon builds what his father King David had on his heart: a permanent dwelling for God (1 Kings 5:5; 1 Chron. 22:7–10; 2 Chron. 6:1–2, 18; Ps. 132:13–14).

After both the tabernacle and the temple were built, the glory of the Lord filled his dwelling place (Exod. 40; 1 Kings 8:10; 2 Chron. 5:13–14).[6] God indeed dwelled among his people! But centuries later, as a consequence of the moral decline of Israel (Judah) and its leaders, God used the Babylonians as the instrument of judgment against his people, sending them into exile. The temple lay in ruins, a physical reminder of the breach between God and his people. God, ever faithful to his covenant, promised a return from exile. Ezekiel painted a glorious and idealized picture of the new temple and the new Jerusalem that would be built when the long years of exile ended, including a return of God's glory (Ezek. 40—48). But did the second temple, built by Haggai and his contemporaries, match this vision? It certainly does not seem so.

Haggai 2:1–9 ends with an expectation that the glory of this second temple will be greater than the glory of Solomon's temple. The temple is indeed finished in 515 BC, but what is its ultimate fate? Unlike Exodus 40, where the glory of God descends on the finished tabernacle, and unlike 1 Kings 8:10 where the glory cloud fills Solomon's temple, no glory cloud is recorded in association with this second temple. If I were a Jew, I would be scratching my head and saying, "God promised to be with us, but I'm not sure what that means exactly. We don't have the ark of the covenant anymore, and we still are living in a land occupied by foreigners. So, where is this greater glory that Haggai predicted?" To be sure, the temple undergoes extensive remodeling around the time of Jesus, but is that the greater glory Haggai proclaimed? Is that when the treasures of the nations come to Jerusalem (v. 7, ESV)? What *did* the Lord mean that the glory of the latter temple would be greater than the glory of the former?

To answer that question, we need to move to the New Testament and explore the connections between the temple and Jesus and his church. Here a surprise awaits: you begin to realize that "future glory" comes in the smallest of packages—a baby born in a manger.[7] It's an inauspicious start, not unlike the building of the second temple. In keeping with the tenor of Haggai 2:3, "Does *he* not seem to you like nothing?!"

John in his Gospel views Jesus as the new temple. Notice John 1:14, "The Word became flesh and made his dwelling among us. We have seen his glory, the glory of the One and Only, who came from the Father, full of grace and truth." This is temple language. Jesus is Immanuel, God with us! In the very next chapter, Jesus clears the temple and declares, "Destroy this temple, and I will raise it again in three days" (2:19). The Jews are thinking literally—Herod's temple—but Jesus is referring to his death and resurrection. Jesus himself becomes the new connecting point between heaven and earth, between God the Father and his people.

But here perhaps is the most amazing and unexpected development. The endpoint is not *Jesus* as the temple but the *church* as temple. Paul asks in 1 Corinthians 3:16, "Don't you know that you yourselves are God's temple and that God's Spirit lives in you?" This is an amplification of Haggai 2:5 that no one would have dreamed of! God choosing to live in a physical structure, sure. But living *within* his people?![8]

To summarize where the New Testament takes the temple imagery, we see that in Jesus the temple is ultimately redefined to include the church. God's people are the place where he now dwells! There is no longer any need for a physical temple. Worship has thus been redefined in Jesus. This is greater glory for certain but a much-amplified version of Haggai 2:9. Also, in an ironic twist, in Jesus glory becomes redefined and preceded by suffering. This then becomes our pattern as his people (Rom. 8:16–27).

Where does it all end up? There's even more glory at the consummation of Jesus' kingdom. Consider the vision of Revelation 21 and 22—the new heavens and new earth. Notice especially 21:22–26 and how it connects with Haggai: "I did not see a temple in the city, because the Lord God Almighty and the Lamb are its temple. The city does not need the sun or the moon to shine on it, for the glory of God gives it light, and the Lamb is its lamp. The nations will walk by its light, and the kings of the earth will bring their splendor into it. On no day will its gates ever be shut, for there will be no night there. The glory and honor of the nations will be brought into it."

Moving toward Application for Tom

Now we ask the question, How does this passage, in light of the gospel, address God's people as saints, sufferers, and sinners? Having listened to Tom's story, how does Haggai 2:1–9 map onto his experience? How should he, to use Eugene Peterson's phrase, "live into God's story"?[9] What connecting points do I have in mind?

Certainly, I would want Tom to gain hope and encouragement in God's presence and persevering love. Like the Jews of Haggai's time, Tom is experiencing consequences from his sin. He looks at his life and is tempted to give up. He looks to the past and sees a string of failures. Perhaps he wonders if the glory has departed for good. Like the recipients of Haggai's prophecy, Tom's hope must be centered on the promise of God's presence and abiding purpose for his people. But unlike the Jews of that time, his hope for the future is not tied to a physical place, the temple. Rather, his hope is found in Jesus, the true temple. The consequences of Tom's sin, while real and difficult, cannot undo the covenant God made with his people through the blood of Jesus. Tom cannot ultimately thwart the transforming and redeeming work of God. "My Spirit remains in you. Do not fear." And Tom has the privilege of experiencing this in far more profound ways than the people of Haggai's day. Truly, as Paul says, "No eye has seen, . . . no mind has conceived, what God has prepared for those who love him" (1 Cor. 2:9, based on Isa. 64:4).

How might this look in conversation with Tom? Here is a potential (albeit idealized) dialogue, using "C" for you, the counselor,[10] and "T" for Tom.

129

C: Tom, I've been thinking about the things you've said to me over the last few weeks. I wonder if we could look at a passage that might speak to some of your struggles.

T: Sure.

C: It's from the book of Haggai. [Opens a Bible to Haggai and hands it to Tom.]

T: Yikes, I think I might have read that once, a long time ago. But I forget what it's about.

C: No problem. Let me briefly set the stage. Do you remember what ultimately happened to the nation of Israel in the Old Testament after years of ongoing sin and rebellion against God?

T: They were booted out of the Promised Land, right?

C: Right! The Babylonians attacked Jerusalem, destroyed the temple, and deported the people. Despite that, God promised that the exiles would return after seventy years. Haggai picks up the action soon after that happens. The people returned and started to rebuild the temple but then stopped when they encountered opposition. In Haggai 1, God stirs up his people to resume the rebuilding efforts, which they do. And that brings us to chapter 2. Can you read Haggai 2:1–9? [Tom reads the passage.] OK, what catches your attention in this passage?

T: I guess one thing is that God speaks to his people in the first place. He hasn't given up on them. He encourages them to keep working despite the setbacks. And he says that he is with them.

C: That's right. It's real evidence of God's faithfulness toward his people despite their sin. But I sense that you're feeling like you've exhausted God's patience, that you've sinned beyond repair, and that your life can never be like it was supposed to be.

T: Yeah, that's true. Some mornings I think, *Why bother anymore?*

C: You know, the people of Haggai's day might have been saying the same thing. Take a look specifically at verse 3— what do you think they were experiencing?

T: God seems to be reading their minds. It sounds like they're remembering what the old temple looked like and how unimpressive this new temple is. Maybe they're thinking that they can never get back to that place of blessing. Yeah, that does resonate some with me. I guess if I were in their shoes I would be tempted to give up the work too.

C: So, what does God say to them to encourage them in their struggle?

T: He tells them, "Be strong and work." He tells them, "I am with you." He tells them not to fear because his Spirit remains among them.

C: Sounds like it's something you need to hear God saying to you as well.

T: Yeah. I really have lost a sense of the Lord's presence. I feel like I'm going through the motions, like there's no real hope for the future. I *am* fearful. I don't want my marriage to end in divorce. But I don't want a shell of a marriage either.

C: What do you think you can expect from God?

T: I'm not sure.

C: What does God promise his disheartened people who are still experiencing the consequences of their (and their ancestors') sin? Take a look at the end of the passage.

T: He makes several promises. He's going to shake up all of creation; he's going to shake the nations; he's going to fill the new temple with glory—glory that surpasses the old temple. Actually, I don't find that as relevant as the earlier part of the passage. So the second temple becomes more glorious; I'm not sure how that relates to me. Is it saying, "Don't worry, things look bad now, but they're going to get better in the future"? Can I really claim that for my life and for my marriage?

C: You raise a good question. No, I don't think it's a blanket promise that magically erases the consequences of sin. God tells his people to work in the present, confident that God's dwelling place would be more glorious in the future. These promises ultimately become true in Jesus

Christ, who is "God with us" in the flesh! But what is God's "address" now? Where does God reside now?

T: Well, it's certainly not the temple. And Jesus is in heaven. I guess you mean that God lives in us through the Holy Spirit.

C: Yes, think about that. The first and second parts of the passage really do hang together. God promises to be with his people. But you get to experience that in a far more glorious way than Haggai and his generation. Jesus has poured out his very presence into your life and the lives of your fellow believers. He indwells his people. You may struggle to feel *him* but he fills *you*. You are his. You are part of his people, marked by his presence. Nothing can take away that identity. The glorious future that Haggai envisioned has begun—you get the foretaste of that in the Spirit.

T: That's helpful for me to hear. I struggle to live in light of that reality. I guess a deeper sense of God's presence would help me move forward in obedience, even if I don't know what my life and marriage will look like in the future. But how do I maintain that awareness of God's presence and his faithfulness?

At this point, the conversation could go in many directions. But perhaps the dialogue suggests some initial steps you could take with Tom. You might have decided to take other steps or highlighted other aspects of Haggai 2 at this point, and that's fine too.

With these connecting points, what are some practical implications for Tom? How does the "gospel trajectory" of Haggai lead to personal transformation? How should Tom's thoughts, emotions, actions, and relationships change in the light of Haggai's text, recast in the gospel? Certainly, I would want Tom to renew his determination to forsake sexual lust and to pursue Sarah with sacrificial love, despite his failure and despite not knowing what "greater glory" might look like in his marriage. He would do this not simply because it is the right thing to do, but because he recognizes where he fits in God's story, a facet of which is seen in Haggai 2. The shape of his obedience could look like a lot of things.

First, Tom could seek greater connection and accountability with the men in his church, recognizing that the church is where God dwells in power and glory. He cannot wage this battle by himself, and he has been most consistent in the past when he has been in honest, accountable relationships. You might say, "Well, duh, that's a no-brainer. You didn't need Haggai to come to that conclusion!" Guess what? I agree with you! Even if you didn't open the Bible, this would be good counsel. But I would also say that the temple imagery from Haggai adds ethical weight for Tom to live in interdependence with others.

Second, I would like to see Tom growing in a "depth" understanding of his struggle with sexual lust. Paul makes a connection between believers as the temple of God's Spirit and the implications for sexual purity in 1 Corinthians 6:18–20: "Flee from sexual immorality. All other sins a man commits are outside his body, but he who sins sexually sins against his own body. Do you not know that your body is a temple of the Holy Spirit, who is in you, whom you have received from God? You are not your own; you were bought at a price. Therefore honor God with your body." This is an echo of Haggai 2:5: "And my Spirit remains among you." God's presence is the foundation and motivation to persevere in the temple-building work (Hag. 2:4).

Notice that completely apart from Haggai 2, we could have used 1 Corinthians 6 to ground Tom's obedience. But I think the temple imagery in 1 Corinthians becomes much deeper and richer, and more connected to the bigger story line of what God is doing, by considering the incredible significance of the temple in the Old Testament. This passage also reveals the high price God paid to dwell among his people. In Haggai you get the picture of treasure and riches pouring into God's temple from the nations. In an ironic twist, God gives the treasure of *himself* to his people and seals the deal with his own blood. When you've been given such a lavish, costly gift, it is meant to be cherished.

What might a snippet of conversation with this emphasis look like?

T: It's been a hard few days. I really feel pulled by sexual temptation. I've definitely been helped by remembering that God's presence and purposes for my life will not fail, but I'm not sure it's enough. Some days it really doesn't feel worth it to obey, particularly when Sarah doesn't seem to have any desire to reconcile.[11]

C: Let's look at another passage that ties in with the meditation you've been doing in Haggai. It picks up the temple theme and connects it directly to the struggle with sexual sin. Let me read 1 Corinthians 6:18–20. [Reads the passage]. Anything hit you?

T: I know this. I should run from sexual temptation. But I'm struggling to *want* to do that!

C: Well, this passage doesn't encourage you to simply "gut it out" in terms of obedience. Paul gives an incredibly personal, relational reason for fleeing sexual immorality and for honoring God with your body.

T: He reminds me that my body is the temple of the Holy Spirit?[12]

C: Right. Think about this: What if, after the temple was built in Haggai, the people started committing all kinds of sexual sin within the temple walls? What would that be like?

T: It would be a gross insult to God, who said he was in their midst. And it would be harmful for faithful followers who had come to the temple to worship God. Pretty much a slap in the face of God who had brought them back from exile and had allowed the temple to be rebuilt.

C: Yes, and it's even more significant for us. Because of Jesus' resurrection and pouring out of his Spirit, the place where you and I worship, the place God dwells, is not stone, bricks, and mortar but flesh and blood! He dwells within us. That's why Paul says earlier in the passage that in committing sexual sin you are actually taking Jesus along as a coparticipant.

T: Wow, I never thought of it like that. It's easy to think it's just me doing these things and forget that I'm a "mobile temple."

Again, you can envision many different conversations with Tom, drawing upon the links between Haggai 2 and 1 Corinthians 6.

One additional thing I might want Tom to see is this: the experience of real glory entails self-sacrifice and suffering. The Jews experienced this as they persevered in their work to rebuild the temple, despite ongoing opposition. Glory could not come without their participation. That pattern of suffering before glory is seen preeminently in Jesus himself. What is true for the King is true for his followers. Many places in the New Testament demonstrate this, including Romans 8:16–27, 2 Corinthians 4, Philippians 3:7–11, and Hebrews 12:1–13, to name a few. Ease, comfort, and escape are not part of the path to greater glory. We want to help Tom recognize these pursuits as glory counterfeits.

Now, are you surprised? Did I "cheat" in my application of Haggai 2:1–9 by moving into other texts?! I don't think so. We are indeed "applying" or "recontextualizing" Haggai's message but not in a way that isolates Haggai 2 from the rest of Scripture. The themes of Haggai 2 carry us to other places in Scripture that enrich our efforts and ultimately ground us in the gospel. In fact, as we become more alert to these connections in the Bible, our flexibility and wisdom grow as we seek to root people's lives in Scripture. Clearly, Haggai is not the only place in Scripture I would want to take Tom over time.

Moving toward Application for Natalie

Unlike Tom or the Jews of Haggai's day, Natalie's struggle does not stem from the consequences of any obvious sin. Rather, she has consistently, prayerfully, and faithfully carried out the ministry to which she believes God called her. Even so, Haggai's message of God's presence and the promise of future glory is one that should resonate with her and give her perspective in the midst of her struggles. Where specifically might some of those points of resonance lie? Let's listen in on a potential conversation.

C: Did you get a chance to look at Haggai 2:1–9 over the last week?

N: I did. It was helpful to read the whole book (as small as it is!). It brought some things back to mind—my pastor preached through the Minor Prophets a couple of years ago.

C: Was there anything that resonated with you? I had asked you to consider the ways in which your experiences and the Jews' experience might have some parallels.

N: Well, one aspect of their experience seems to be a sense of incompleteness.

C: What do you mean?

N: They looked at the new temple under construction and longed for something more. Longed for the way it used to be. Longed for something more glorious than what they saw now. Their discouragement seems evident in the way God responds to them in verse 3. Maybe they were thinking, *Is this as good as it gets?*

C: How does that relate to you?

N: It's not so much that I'm looking backward, pining for the glory days. I'm not sure those were "glory days"! It's more that I'm dissatisfied with the present. I want to see something more glorious happen. I am grateful for the impact I see, like better overall health for my young patients, but I long for so much more for them. Truthfully, I had hoped there would be more to show for my labors over the years.

C: I'm sure it *was* difficult for the Jews to persevere in the work of temple building, given its appearance. So, in the absence of present glory, what did God promise the Jews?

N: God said he was present with them and that his Spirit remained among them. And he promised future glory for the temple.

C: So, when did that happen?

N: Well, I'm not sure. Verses 6–8 seem to suggest that material riches will be brought from the nations to adorn the temple. But you've been drumming into my head over the last few weeks the need to connect any passage with Christ [smiles], so I suspect something more is in view.

C: Let me read John 1:14: "The Word became flesh and made his dwelling among us. We have seen his glory, the glory of the One and Only, who came from the Father, full of grace and truth." Notice the temple ("dwelling") language here.

N: So, the greater glory is not seen in the physical temple but in Jesus himself.

C: Yes—and that is good news. But is that the end of the story? Is what we see now as good as it gets? Have we experienced the full measure of future glory?

N: It's hard to imagine that's true when I look around my neighborhood.

C: That's right. Even we postresurrection believers have not yet experienced the full measure of glory. Glory is still under construction, within us and outside of us in our world. I think that's why Paul uses the phrase, "Christ in you, the *hope* of glory" in Colossians 1:27. We and all of God's creation will not experience that full renewal and glory until Jesus returns.

N: Are you saying I'm expecting too much of the future in the present?

C: I think it's simply that you have had a taste of Christ's glory already and you long for more. To use the language of Paul in Romans 8:18–25, you "groan" as you wait expectantly for the full measure of restoration to come. Theologians call this the tension between the "already" and the "not yet" of the kingdom.

N: But how do I live with contentment in that place of tension?

There are multiple ways to answer Natalie's question. First, I might suggest that she make the assurance of "future glory" part of her prayer for the kingdom to come more fully in her place of service.[13] But I would urge her not to overlook a day in which the kingdom comes in small ways. This is reminiscent of the Lord's encouragement to Zechariah (Haggai's contemporary) regarding the beginnings of the second temple: "The hands of Zerubbabel have laid the foundation of this temple; his hands will also complete it. . . . . Who despises the day of small things? Men will rejoice when they see the plumb line in the hand of Zerubbabel" (Zech. 4:9–10). I would encourage Natalie to journal, or at least to incorporate into her prayer life, a daily record of the smallest glimpses of future glory evident in her medical practice now.

Secondly, I want her to see the crucial part she plays in God's promised future glory. In Haggai's day, building the temple was critical to the building of God's kingdom ("God's people in God's place under God's rule"). The kingdom had a geographical center, and its centerpiece was the temple. But in the New Testament, "place" becomes "person" as Jesus claims the temple imagery for himself and his people. Now where the people of God are, you find the presence of the kingdom because the King indwells his church by his Spirit. Rather than seeing the temple as the sacred place to which the nations and their treasures stream (Hag. 2:7; Isa. 61), the new temple (the church) moves into the world so that it might "be filled with the knowledge of the glory of the LORD, as the waters cover the sea" (Hab. 2:14). Natalie's practice is a "kingdom outpost." She incarnates the presence of God to a glory-starved neighborhood. How about that for giving perspective on a day when she treats one sore throat after another?!

Thirdly, it's important for Natalie to see that God's presence grounds this kingdom-building work (Hag. 2:4–5). His presence is the antidote to battle weariness and fatigue—"'Be strong . . . and work. For I am with you,' declares the LORD Almighty." In a similar fashion, Jesus commissions his disciples in Matthew 28:19–20, grounding the task in his presence. The King, by his Spirit, accompanies and empowers his ambassadors. He does not leave his children alone. Natalie can draw encouragement from meditating on the reality of Christ's presence with her in the midst of the most trying days, weeks, and months of her medical practice.

Notice that I did not specifically counsel Natalie as to whether she should continue in the urban clinic, practice medicine elsewhere, or leave medicine to pursue full-time church ministry. No doubt such a discussion is important, but helping Natalie to see her current situation through a gospel lens is a crucial prerequisite for considering other vocational options. Using Haggai to give Natalie a kingdom-centered perspective on her problems may provide the clarification needed for the next step, whether it means persevering in her current work or moving elsewhere. Sometimes God's call is simply for our attitudes to reflect his perspective, and sometimes the call is for our attitudes *and* our situations to change.

Conclusion

I hope that you have gotten a better sense of how to approach both Haggai and specific people, and that you have gained some confidence in how to help Tom and Natalie (or anyone you know!) live in the plotline of Haggai as it comes to fruition in Jesus Christ and his church. I have used Haggai to give a Christ-centered perspective to their struggles. This leads to wise changes in the motivations, thinking, emotions, and actions of these two individuals. In this sense, connecting Scripture with life is as much (Spirit-dependent) art as it is (Spirit-dependent) science. The questions and categories I have given you are not foolproof. They are tools to guide you in studying Scripture and people, but you need to use them in utter dependence on God's Spirit to give you his wisdom in the moment (Col. 1:6).

Discussion Questions

1. Think of someone you are caring for right now. How might you use Haggai 2:1–9 to minister to him or her?
2. What are the similarities and differences in the way Haggai was used with Tom and with Natalie?
3. Now that you have seen the model in action, what questions do you have about the task of connecting Scripture to real life?

CHAPTER 10

Tom, Natalie, and the New Testament

In the previous chapter you saw how a single passage from the Old Testament could connect with two people with very different experiences and struggles. In this chapter we will minister to Tom and Natalie again, this time using a New Testament text: Mark 1:40–45, the encounter between Jesus and a leper. (I know you may be thinking, *Whew, I'm glad he didn't choose Revelation 16!*) As with Haggai, this choice is not like magically pulling a rabbit from a hat. I have some baseline familiarity with this text, having studied it and preached on it in the past. I also could have considered the themes of Tom's or Natalie's lives and asked, "What New Testament passage(s) might speak to their experiences as saints, sufferers, and sinners?" If I had, I would likely have ended up with different texts for each person. Instead, I am starting with a given text and wrestling with how it specifically might help *both* Tom and Natalie.

Reading (Interpreting) Mark 1:40–45

I will again use the questions from chapter 7 to guide our understanding of this passage in Mark. I encourage you to read a brief introduction to the Gospel of Mark or skim the book before interacting with the questions I outline below. Take a look at Mark 1:40–45:

A man with leprosy came to him and begged him on his knees, "If you are willing, you can make me clean." Filled with compassion, Jesus reached out his hand and touched the man. "I am willing," he said. "Be clean!" Immediately the leprosy left him and he was cured. Jesus sent him away at once with a strong warning: "See that you don't tell this to anyone. But go, show yourself to the priest and offer the sacrifices that Moses commanded for your cleansing, as a testimony to them." Instead he went out and began to talk freely, spreading the news. As a result, Jesus could no longer enter a town openly but stayed outside in lonely places. Yet the people still came to him from everywhere.

Original Context

As with Haggai, we want to ask what had happened in redemptive history at the time the story takes place.[1] We can build upon our work in the last chapter. Although the postexilic community completed the temple and rebuilt the walls of Jerusalem, they continued to be ruled by a succession of foreigners. Temple-based worship and increased concern for Torah (the Law) marked community life, but God's promise to restore the Davidic kingdom (Jer. 23:5–6; 30; Ezek. 34; 37:15–28) remained unfulfilled. Messianic hopes grew during this period. When would God act decisively to restore his kingdom through Israel?

With that awareness, the next step is to address the question, What do you think God was trying to communicate to his people at this particular point in redemptive history? That is, what would you judge the main theme or point?[2] Remember, whether you have studied this passage for hours or read it carefully for the first time this morning, during your devotions, you are able to answer this question with the Spirit's help!

So, with five minutes of prayerful reflection, what should you see? That Jesus is willing and able to heal the leper. He cleanses the shameful, unclean outcasts of society. Simple! That is a true understanding of the passage, and it equips you to make meaningful connections with Tom and Natalie's lives.

Of course, my burden is to help you become even better students of Scripture and people. That's not all there is to see in this passage! What you will read below is my *cumulative* meditation on the story. Just as I would expect my knowledge of Tom and Natalie to grow the more time I spend with them, the same is true for this passage. Such effort can yield additional connections between Mark's Gospel and Tom and Natalie's stories. So, let's stretch out the accordion and explore the treasures Mark offers, knowing that we won't bring all these observations to either Tom or Natalie in any one sitting.

First, notice that Mark places this account at the end of a series of "kingdom activities" of Jesus (1:21–39). These accounts follow on the heels of Jesus' proclamation, in 1:15, "The kingdom of God is near. Repent and believe the good news!" It's as though Mark is saying, "Here is what the coming of the kingdom looks like: overthrowing demons, healing the sick, prayer, preaching, and [in our passage] cleansing from leprosy." This ties in with 1:1, where Mark introduces his Gospel: "The beginning of the gospel[3] about Jesus Christ, the Son of God." Mark's concern is to highlight the good news that a new king, God's Son Jesus, has come on the scene. He stands in contrast to both the Roman emperor *and* the revolutionary Messiah of Jewish expectations. Mark seeks to proclaim the identity of King Jesus and the nature of his reign. His burden is to show that the true King has come.

We approach Mark 1:40–45 within that literary context. What do you notice in the details of the passage? In verse 40 we see that the leper, contrary to Jewish law that required lepers to stay away from others for fear of contamination (Lev. 13:45–46),[4] approaches Jesus, convinced that Jesus *could* heal him but not convinced that Jesus *would* or wanted to do so.

Verses 41–42 reveal Jesus' amazing response to the leper's impassioned plea for healing. Mark notes that Jesus was "filled with compassion." It's clear that Jesus does not usher in his kingdom in a dutiful, detached kind of way. He deeply feels the suffering of his people. He is moved by their plight. Then a shocking thing happens: Jesus stretches out his hand and *touches* the leper! Didn't Jesus know that to touch someone unclean would make *him* unclean (Lev. 5:3)? And why did he have to touch him anyhow? He healed many others by merely speaking a word. What's going on here? Certainly his touch demonstrates his compassion and his willingness to rub shoulders with the untouchables of society. Throughout the Gospels we see Jesus hanging out with "notorious sinners" and the outcasts of Jewish society by virtue of disease or demon possession. But perhaps there's something more.

Rather than becoming unclean by touching the leper, as any other human being would, Jesus possesses a "contagious cleanness."[5] Here is the spiritual equivalent of the Midas touch at work. He demonstrates his authority over impurity and uncleanness as he heals the leper. The true King heals even the most hopeless case, something really only God can do (Num. 12; 2 Kings 5:7).

This healing by Jesus calls to mind J. R. R. Tolkien's chapter from *The Return of the King,* entitled "The Houses of Healing."[6] The backdrop for this chapter is the battle for Minas Tirith, the great city of the realm of Gondor. Three main characters, Faramir (the son of Gondor's now dead acting ruler), Eowyn (the maiden warrior from the realm of Rohan), and Merry (a hobbit), were gravely wounded in battle and taken to a place where Gondor's healers seek to help them. But their wounds are too serious and they lay dying.

Tolkien writes, "Then an old wife, Ioreth, the eldest of the women who served in that house, looking on the fair face of Faramir, wept, for all the people loved him. And she said: 'Alas! if he should die. Would that there were kings in Gondor, as there were once upon a time, they say! For it is said in old lore: *The hands of the king are the hands of a healer.* And so the rightful king could ever be known.'"[7]

The great wizard Gandalf confirmed the healer's words, "It is only in the coming of Aragorn that any hope remains for the sick that lie in the House."[8]

Unbeknownst to the woman, Gondor's long-anticipated king, Aragorn, had returned in victory, ultimately to ascend the throne that had been unoccupied for so long. And so Aragorn comes to the Houses of Healing and brings his healing touch first to Faramir, then Eowyn, and finally Merry. I love the way Tolkien words the healing of Eowyn: "'Awake, Eowyn, Lady of Rohan!' said Aragorn again, and he took her right hand in his and felt it warm with life returning. 'Awake! The shadow is gone and all darkness is washed clean!'"[9] Indeed, the shadow was banished; the king had returned! And Aragorn's identity as king was revealed in his ability to heal the mortally wounded.

Do you see the parallels with Jesus? Mark begins his Gospel with the conclusion he wants his readers to make about Jesus' identity: He is the Messiah, the Son of God. His actions demonstrate that Jesus is no pretender to the throne. He has power to cleanse even leprosy, a kind of living death. He is able to restore wholeness to what is broken and ruined by the fall.

But the passage doesn't end with the healing of the leper. Why did Mark add the details of verses 43–45? I believe it has to do with the *way* in which Jesus brings his kingdom to earth. This is *not* a spectacular miracle to pump up messianic expectations to overthrow the Roman government. No, this King, while clearly demonstrating his authority in every way, shows that humility, lowliness, loneliness, and suffering are the currency of the kingdom. Where do we see this?

In verses 43–44a Jesus sends the healed leper away with a strong warning, "See that you don't tell this to anyone." Huh?! Why suppress the good news? Although not characteristic of every miracle Jesus does, this command is not an unusual one— see Mark 5:43; 7:36; Matthew 9:30; and Luke 4:41. But why this "messianic secret"?[10] Matthew 12:16–21 gives an important clue as to why Jesus gave these strict warnings. Matthew says it was "to fulfill what was spoken through the prophet Isaiah: 'Here is my servant whom I have chosen, the one I love, in whom I delight; I will put my Spirit on him, and he will proclaim justice to the nations. He will not quarrel or cry out; no one will hear his voice in the streets.'"

Jesus' ministry is like that of a "stealth bomber." He *will* accomplish his mission to destroy the ultimate enemies of sin and death, but he will do it in a way that is not so obvious (and in fact is ultimately counterintuitive in the highest degree—through death on a cross!). In other words, Jesus does not permit an announcement of his kingdom in a way that draws attention to himself; it might give people the wrong idea of just how he was going to usher in his kingdom.

Jesus' humility is further seen in verse 44b. He tells the healed leper to adhere to the Mosaic law for the cleansing of those healed with leprosy/infectious skin diseases by going to the priest and offering the prescribed sacrifices (see Lev. 14:1–32).[11] But even as Jesus adheres to and fulfills the law as the servant of the Lord, he supersedes the law. How so? Notice that the purity laws themselves had no power to cleanse, unlike Jesus who has both the willingness and the power to cleanse. The priest could only pronounce a person clean or unclean; he had no power in himself to change the actual status of a person from unclean to clean. He had no power in himself to restore the unclean one to fellowship within the community. Only Jesus, God in the flesh, could accomplish this change of status.

What happened next? Could the cleansed leper keep a secret? Did he go to the priest and complete the requirements for his full restoration before God and others? No, he "began to talk freely, spreading the news." What was the result for Jesus? The first-century Palestinian equivalent of paparazzi mobbing a celebrity. Mark records that Jesus "could no longer enter a town openly but stayed outside in lonely places" (v. 45). Jesus' restoration of the leper meant Jesus' own exclusion from community life. The passage begins with the leper required by law to live in isolation from others; the passage ends with Jesus having to remain in those same lonely places. Jesus really does "trade places" with the leper.[12]

You might call this a "reversal rehearsal" of sorts. It's quite possible that Mark is foreshadowing the ultimate reversal of fortune that takes place for Jesus at the cross. This servant humility is expressed by Jesus himself in Mark 10:45: "For even the Son of Man did not come to be served, but to serve, and to give his life as a ransom for many." In this passage Jesus gives up comfort and community life as a result of serving and healing the leper. But this is only the beginning. Mark's Gospel highlights the fact that the way of the kingdom is the way of the cross.[13]

Given this detailed study of the text, I would summarize the passage this way: "Jesus is the King who is willing and able to cleanse those who are unclean—at his own expense." Of course, this is not the only way to summarize the passage, but it captures the central thrust of the narrative as well as the more subtle fore-shadowing of Jesus' suffering at the end of the passage, which becomes more explicit as Mark progresses.

Now we need to ask what response we think the author intended. How might this passage have affected the lives of the original hearers/readers? What response might result from hear-ing God's message? Of course, this response is tied to the themes and emphases of Mark's Gospel as a whole, which center on the identity and kingdom mission of Jesus, and the implications for his followers.

If I were to give a title for Mark, it would be "The Author-ity and Suffering of the True King." "Mark wants his readers to understand that Jesus is the Son of God, but especially the *suffer-ing* Son of God. Mark also shows that Christians must walk the same road as Jesus—the way of humility, of suffering, and even, should it be necessary, of death."[14]

So Mark, writing 1:40–45, would prompt amazement and worship in his readers as they encounter the King who comes with authority to cleanse. It might also prompt readers to ask, "If the Son of God suffers and dies on his way to bring cleansing (a foreshadowing of which appears in the passage), what practical steps of cross-centered obedience should I take? What steps of self-denial should I pursue?" Finally, if Mark directs his Gospel toward suffering Christians in Rome, a hypothesis that many bib-lical scholars propose, Mark's portrait of Jesus would encourage them to persevere, following in the footsteps of their Savior.

Expanded (Redemptive-Historical) Context

The next step is to put the passage in the larger context of Scripture, beginning with the question, Why was this passage par-ticularly important at the time it was written? In other words, how does this passage contribute to God's progressive revelation?

Have you ever anticipated an event for years? Have you ever wished that something you were fairly certain would happen in the future could happen right here, right now? Perhaps it was the beginning of a specific career. Or getting married. Or buying a house. The longer we wait for something, the more expectation builds, and the more vivid our imaginations become regarding the fulfillment of our desires.

The Jews anticipated, longed for, and prayed for the coming of the Messiah and, with him, the decisive in-breaking of God's rule on earth. Mark surely presents God's kingdom coming with decisive power through Jesus. But such fulfilled expectations are coupled with suffering and crucifixion. This flies in the face of both Jewish and Greco-Roman expectations of kingship. So Mark wrote his Gospel to proclaim that Jesus, the healer, the exorcist, the One who cleanses the unclean, the teacher and preacher, the crucified and resurrected One, is the Son of God, the true King. Mark's main burden is to proclaim the identity, authority, and mission of Jesus to an early church in the grip of persecution. Jesus is the true King (ultimate victory!), but the way of his kingdom involves suffering as a prelude to glory (perseverance and humility in suffering!).

We now need to ask, How does the main theme of the passage connect with Scripture written earlier and later in redemptive history?[15] In this step we once again draw upon our overall knowledge of Scripture; we use cross-references; we do word, concept, and theme studies using concordances, Bible programs, or other resources such as the *Dictionary of Biblical Imagery*. Of course, you are much more likely to do extensive study of this kind if you are preparing to lead a Bible study than if you are counseling someone. You're not going to say to your counselee, "Uh, could we reschedule our appointment? I haven't finished looking up the cross-references to the passage I asked you to read for this week!" Rather, your personal devotions and your preparations for Bible study may do double duty. That is, because you have lived with a particular passage, it is more likely that you will use it as you meet one-on-one with someone. You have increased the routes you can use to connect Scripture with someone's life.

Consider the metaphor of driving in an unfamiliar city. At first you are tethered to a map, Internet-based driving directions, or your GPS. But the more driving you do, the more familiar you become with the connections between different parts of the city.

In fact, if you find yourself in less-familiar territory, you might figure out where to go based on the growing web of directions in your head.

Using Scripture in ministry is a lot like that. The more familiar you become with how passages (routes) connect—and this is a process that occurs over time—the greater your flexibility when you face a detour or some other event that requires a route change. You will draw from accumulated wisdom—and it may be a passage you studied intently several years ago!

The same growth in knowledge and wisdom should occur in your relationships with people. Although you may be able to say something helpful after talking with a person for thirty minutes, consider what "relational capital" has been built when you have spent twenty hours with the person in several different contexts. Based on this "extended study," you have more options, more connecting points with the person's life. Our goal is always greater depth of understanding and skill with people and with Scripture, even as we ask the Spirit to use us at *any* point along the journey.

So, what connections with Mark 1:40–45 can we explore over minutes, hours, and perhaps years of study that will serve us well in personal ministry? An appropriate place to begin would be passages that speak of the clean vs. unclean distinction because this seems central to the passage.[16] Type in "clean" or "unclean" in a Bible program or look it up in a concordance, and you will find Leviticus full of such references, more than any other book in the Bible. As we saw earlier, Leviticus 13:39 and 14:1–32 explain the state of leprosy and its regulation within the community, including the process of cleansing from this condition. But notice that this falls within a larger section of Leviticus dealing with the clean/unclean distinction. Many things are considered "unclean" or "impure" in the Old Testament, including skin diseases (Lev. 13—14), mildew in buildings (Lev. 14), discharge from the sexual organs (Lev. 15), women who have given birth (Lev. 12), dead bodies (Num. 5:2; 9:6–7; 19:11, 13), and certain animals (Lev. 11).

Now you may think, *What's the big deal? Why all the fuss about what is clean and what is unclean?* The answer lies in the connection between uncleanness and guilt before God. Becoming unclean meant separation from God and his people. Restoration from uncleanness required sacrifice, specifically sacrifices for sin or guilt (Lev. 5:2–3, 5–6). The reason for this is found in Leviticus 11:44–45: "I am the LORD your God; consecrate yourselves and be holy, because I am holy. Do not make yourselves unclean by any creature that moves about on the ground. I am the LORD who brought you up out of Egypt to be your God; therefore be holy, because I am holy." A similar command is found in Leviticus 15:31: "You must keep the Israelites separate from things that make them unclean, so they will not die in their uncleanness for defiling my dwelling place, which is among them."

The distinction between clean and unclean was not merely hygienic or ceremonial but ethical and moral. In reality, the distinction between clean and unclean showed the true gulf that existed between God and humanity. How can the holy dwell with the unholy? How can the One who is perfectly clean live among those who are always at risk of uncleanness? No wonder God provided the sacrificial system as a necessary means of cleansing and atonement!

Ezekiel develops the "location" and "agent" of cleansing in Ezekiel 36:24–27: "For I will take you out of the nations; I will gather you from all the countries and bring you back into your own land. I will sprinkle clean water on you, and you will be clean; I will cleanse you from all your impurities and from all your idols. I will give you a new heart and put a new spirit in you; I will remove from you your heart of stone and give you a heart of flesh. And I will put my Spirit in you and move you to follow my decrees and be careful to keep my laws." The location of cleansing is the heart; the agent of that cleansing is God himself. I find it interesting that the sacrificial system is not mentioned here as part of the solution. As will become very clear in the New Testament, the blood of sacrifices can never ultimately take away the uncleanness of sin.

But when would this "heart transplant" happen? Who will cure God's people of their backsliding, impurity, and uncleanness?

Mark answers emphatically: Jesus the Messiah, the Son of God. He is a king bent not on external cleansing—driving the unclean Romans out of the land—but on the restoration and purification of the very image of God through a Spirit-wrought heart change.[17] But it is a cleansing for God's people that comes at the cost of Jesus' own blood shed on the cross. The leper's condition is no mere external defilement. In reality, he is Everyman—unclean on the inside as well, separated from God and others, with no hope for restoration apart from the compassion and power of Jesus. A cleansed leper still faces the fate of death. Only Jesus can rescue him (and us) from that ultimate defilement.

Where do other New Testament writers take this idea of clean and unclean? How is the cleansing Jesus performs in Mark 1 further developed by other biblical authors, in light of the cross and resurrection? We can think in two broad categories: restoration of relationship with God (the vertical dimension) and relationships with one another (the horizontal dimension).

Regarding the vertical dimension, the book of Hebrews contrasts the sacrificial system with the work of Christ. Consider the following passages:

> The blood of goats and bulls and the ashes of a heifer sprinkled on those who are ceremonially unclean sanctify them so that they are outwardly clean. How much more, then, will the blood of Christ, who through the eternal Spirit offered himself unblemished to God, cleanse our consciences from acts that lead to death, so that we may serve the living God! (9:13–14)

> The law is only a shadow of the good things that are coming—not the realities themselves. For this reason it can never, by the same sacrifices repeated endlessly year after year, make perfect those who draw near to worship. If it could, would they not have stopped being offered? For the worshipers would have been cleansed once for all, and would no longer have felt guilty for their sins. But those sacrifices are an annual reminder of sins, because it is impossible for the blood of bulls and goats to take away sins. (10:1–4)

Day after day every priest stands and performs his religious
duties; again and again he offers the same sacrifices, which
can never take away sins. But when this priest [Jesus] had
offered for all time one sacrifice for sins, he sat down at
the right hand of God. Since that time he waits for his
enemies to be made his footstool, because by one sacrifice
he has made perfect forever those who are being made holy.
(10:11–14)

The author of Hebrews highlights the once-for-all cleansing
that Jesus brings through the sacrifice of his own blood. The sacrificial system could regulate uncleanness and sin, but it could
not remove it. Only the blood of the ultimate sacrifice, God's
own Son, accomplishes that. Such cleansing frees us to live with a
clean conscience, knowing that the penalty for sin has been paid.
It invites confidence that "if we confess our sins, he is faithful and
just and will forgive us our sins and purify [i.e., cleanse] us from
all unrighteousness" (1 John 1:9).

Not only is Jesus the perfect sacrifice who brings once-for-all
cleansing, his work is ongoing as our Great High Priest (Heb. 4:14–
16; 7:24–26). Not only is Jesus the King who inaugurates his kingdom through his own death and resurrection (as Mark reveals), he
also lives to intercede for his people (as Hebrews reveals).

What about the horizontal dimension? Not only has Jesus'
cleansing brought restoration between God and his people, this
cleansing also impacts relationships with one another in the
church. It has community implications. If the barrier between
God and man has been addressed through the atoning work of
Jesus, how can barriers between God's people remain? More specifically, a question facing the early church was what to do about
the Gentiles who were turning to Jesus. After all, Gentiles were
ceremonially unclean!

But the book of Acts demonstrates that *all* who call upon the
name of the Lord Jesus receive forgiveness and the gift of the
Holy Spirit (Acts 10—11; 15). Paul puts it this way in Galatians
3:26–29: "You are all sons of God through faith in Christ Jesus,
for all of you who were baptized into Christ have clothed yourselves with Christ. There is neither Jew nor Greek, slave nor free,

male nor female, for you are all one in Christ Jesus. If you belong to Christ, then you are Abraham's seed, and heirs according to the promise." No longer are there "outsiders" and "insiders," clean or unclean in Jesus' kingdom. The gravity of the kingdom pulls toward the breaching of relational barriers, toward engagement with those who might be considered "unclean."

Another interpersonal connection centers on the "cost" of cleansing the unclean. We see how costly our cleansing is for Jesus, as Mark (and the other Gospels) narrate his march to the cross. But there are also implications for the servants of the King as we live in community. We, too, are called to live sacrificially in our roles as "ministers of reconciliation" (2 Cor. 5:18). In this sense, we are "agents of cleansing" whose job description parallels our Savior's pattern of service. Consider what the author of Hebrews says: "And so Jesus also suffered outside the city gate to make the people holy through his own blood. Let us, then, go to him outside the camp, bearing the disgrace he bore" (13:12–13). How much we are like James and John in Mark 10, requesting places of honor and power in Jesus' kingdom! How much we need to hear Jesus' words to them afresh, "You don't know what you are asking. . . . For even the Son of Man did not come to be served, but to serve, and to give his life as a ransom for many" (10:38, 45).

There is a flow or progression to the redemptive-historical work. It's not simply a collection of isolated texts on cleansing but a discernible story line to which Mark 1:40–45 adds its voice. The primary goal is not to do an exhaustive topical study on "clean/ unclean" distinctions in Scripture but to notice how the clean/ unclean plotline progresses and develops over time in redemptive history.

If you feel overwhelmed by all these connections, remember that it's a cumulative process. Remember that with only Mark 1:40–45 in hand, you still have much to give Tom or Natalie. With an awareness of how Mark connects with other places in Scripture, you have even more. Even a few minutes of reflection, cross-reference checking, or reading your study Bible margin notes should take you on a helpful journey. Trust that God will use your efforts at reading Scripture and reading people whatever your level of understanding, even as you push for deeper engagement.

Moving toward Application with Tom

As we did with Haggai, how might we approach Tom using Mark 1:40–45? How does the theme of this passage—"Jesus is the King who is willing and able to cleanse—at his own expense"— minister to Tom? How does Mark 1:40–45 secure his identity, shape his suffering, and address his sin? Again, I won't artificially separate those three categories in my approach. Let's pick up the conversation near the end of an appointment.

C: Tom, it seems that part of your daily experience is living with an ongoing sense of guilt or shame.

T: Yeah. I mean, I *know* God forgives me. But this sense of "dirtiness" keeps hanging on, especially living with Sarah. Not that she keeps bringing up my sins in every conversation, but seeing her every day and knowing she's so unhappy reminds me of all my failures and inadequacies as a husband.

C: What else contributes to that lingering sense of shame?

T: My job situation. This has always been a struggle. I remember my tenth-year high school reunion. Most of my friends had finished college or grad school and were in professional vocations. What could I say? "Yeah, I became a Christian, got my girlfriend pregnant, dropped out of college, and now I'm in a dead-end job. Great to see you, too."

C: That's quite a memory. It sounds like this sense of failure and shame go right down to your core.

T: Yeah, that's true. It makes it hard even to approach God sometimes.

C: Can we look at a passage together that might address some aspects of what you are experiencing?[18]

T: Sure. It's not in *Zephaniah* is it? [Smiles]

C: No, we're in the New Testament this time. It's Mark 1:40–45. Would you read the passage? [Tom reads.] OK, what do you notice?

T: That he actually touched the leper. I mean, that was against the law, right? He's risking contamination to heal this guy.

C: That's right. So, what do you think Jesus' attitude is toward this outcast?

T: Jesus moves toward him when everyone else would run away. He tells the leper, "I am willing."

C: Do you sense that same attitude in Jesus toward you?

T: Well, sort of. I mean, I *know* he's willing to forgive, to cleanse. But I guess if I'm honest, I envision him thinking, *Hmmph. Messed up again?! Can't you get your act together? OK, I'll reach out to you again* this *time.*

C: I'm not surprised by that. If we feel disapproval and shame before other people consistently, it's likely to be there in our view of God, too. I want you to camp out in this passage for the next week, focusing on the compassion of Jesus and his willingness to cleanse the leper. He is willing and able to cleanse you, too, Tom. No additional sacrificial system is necessary. There are no other hoops to jump through. I want you to think about the implications of these truths for your relationship with God and with others. In other words, how would your life look different if you grabbed hold of the cleansing from guilt and shame that Jesus offers you? One thing that might stimulate your thinking about the implications comes from a passage in Hebrews: "Therefore, brothers, since we have confidence to enter the Most Holy Place by the blood of Jesus, by a new and living way opened for us through the curtain, that is, his body, and since we have a great priest over the house of God, let us draw near to God with a sincere heart in full assurance of faith, having our hearts sprinkled to cleanse us from a guilty conscience and having our bodies washed with pure water" (10:19–22).

T: I'd really like to experience that kind of freedom. I want more of that confidence and assurance before God.

In recognition of Jesus' compassion, will Tom, like the leper, come (and keep coming!) to Jesus?[19] He is the only one who can bring healing. He is the only one who can cleanse from what defiles. He takes away our guilt and bears our shame on the cross. And as our risen and exalted Great High Priest, Jesus invites

Tom, "Come." I would love Tom to take to heart the words of the hymn, "Come Ye Sinners, Poor and Wretched":[20]

> Come, ye sinners, poor and wretched, weak and wounded,
>   sick and sore;
> Jesus ready stands to save you, full of pity joined with pow'r;
> He is able, he is able, he is able,
> He is willing; doubt no more; he is willing; doubt no more.
>   (v. 1)
> Come, ye weary, heavy laden, bruised and broken by the fall;
> If you tarry till you're better, you will never come at all:
> Not the righteous, not the righteous, not the righteous—
> Sinners Jesus came to call; sinners Jesus came to call. (v. 3)

An increased sense of cleansing and freedom before God should also extend to Tom's relationships with others, particularly Sarah. While this does not guarantee that Tom's relationship with Sarah will be restored, it does give Tom humble confidence to move toward Sarah in hope, despite her current ambivalence. He does not have to cry out "Unclean, unclean!" as he approaches her, though he must remain sensitive to the ways in which he has wounded her. His identity as a cleansed servant-son of the King frees him to move into relationships where insecurity and conflict exist. It also gives him courage to tackle head-on the disappointments of his job situation, which, over time, may have undercut his sense of purpose and identity as a man and husband.

Tom would also benefit from considering the cost of his cleansing as a reason to persevere in obedience. He partakes of the kingdom because the King suffers and dies, and Mark 1:40–45 gives just a hint of that. Here's how the conversation might sound.

C: We've been talking about the implications of your cleansing, and one of the things you said was, "It motivates me to live true to my cleansed status. Using pornography goes against the grain of my identity in Christ as a cleansed man." I agree with that. Think about when we've just bathed one of our children. The last thing we want him or her to do is go out and play in the mud (although it happens!). Rather, we want them to live with an awareness that they are clean. (Of course, the analogy breaks down there because my children, at least, remain "clean" all of about an hour or two!) But can I suggest another motivation for obedience? [Tom nods.] Did cleansing the leper cost Jesus anything?

T: Well, I guess he risked being unclean by touching the leper. So he risked being lumped in with the outcasts of society. He definitely was criticized for being a friend of tax collectors and sinners.

C: That's true. And that risk becomes a kind of reality by the end of the passage. What do you see happening there?

T: The leper didn't do what Jesus commanded him to do. Instead he went out and told everyone about his healing. And it says that, as a result, Jesus had to stay outside the town limits, in lonely places.

C: How does that compare to the leper's position?

T: I guess the leper may have gotten back into social life, although he never did participate in the required sacrifices. He started as an outcast and ended as a restored member of the community. Seems like the opposite for Jesus.

C: Good eyes! I think that's right. Although Jesus was not technically unclean at this point, his cleansing ministry led here to a kind of separation from community life. It is true that the people came out to him, but he stayed in the "lonely places." I think that's a foreshadowing of what Jesus' mission was going to cost him. At the cross Jesus was cut off from his people, cut off from even the Father. He became utterly defiled, so that you and I might be cleansed.

T: That's really humbling to think about. I don't consider that the way I should in the midst of sexual temptation. When you're given a wonderful, costly gift, you want to cherish it, not squander it.

C: Yes. Remember that passage we looked at in 1 Corinthians 6? We had talked about the temple imagery, the fact that you have the Holy Spirit living within you, which is a very personal deterrent to sin. But Paul also uses the cost of redemption as a motive for sexual purity in verses 19b–20: "You are not your own; you were bought at a price. Therefore honor God with your body."[21]

What are some other points of connection? In an indirect way this passage offers Tom the ultimate hope for lasting change in the area of sexual purity. Jesus' cleansing of the leper was a precursor to the resurrection, bringing someone who was functionally dead—spiritually, physically, and socially—back to life. The mighty power of the same Spirit who raised Jesus from the dead is now at work in Tom, combating his current discouragement and fighting his temptations to "exchange" the reality of his cleansing for short-term pornographic pleasures.

This passage, particularly when coupled with Mark 7:1–23, would help Tom understand that cleansing (and the ongoing battle with sin) occurs at the level of the heart. While I want Tom to rest in the once-for-all cleansing that Jesus gives him, I also want him to fight against the deeper roots of his discontent that have led to the escape of pornography, including his idealized dream for married life, his discomfort with relational conflict, and his insecurity and fear about his adequacy as a husband and provider. Tom has spoken about pornography as a place of control (and perhaps safety) to which he retreats. Ongoing work with Tom will address these deeper desires and fears and frame them within the cleansing from guilt and shame that Jesus provides.

Let me close this section by returning to Tolkien's account of the Houses of Healing. Consider Faramir's response to Aragorn's healing: "Suddenly Faramir stirred, and he opened his eyes, and he looked on Aragorn who bent over him; and a light of knowledge and love was kindled in his eyes, and he spoke softly, 'My lord you called me. I come. What does the king command?' 'Walk no more in the shadows, but awake!' said Aragorn. 'You are weary. Rest awhile, and take food, and be ready when I return.' 'I will, lord,' said Faramir, 'For who would lie idle when the king has returned?'"[22]

Who would lie idle when the king has returned? Indeed! Jesus' cleansing is a catalyst for action![23] The coming of the kingdom is a call to radical discipleship until the King returns. Moving toward Sarah in simple acts of sacrificial love; consistently praying with her that Jesus' kingdom priorities would characterize their marriage and family life; reestablishing accountability relationships with men in the church; forsaking the lure of financial security, confident in cleansing and in his possession of the kingdom:[24] all of these may be specific markers of growth in Tom's life. In times of hardship, Tom's life has had a wistful, regretful backward glance: "If only I had ____." Instead of his past failures I want him to see the past, present, and future work of God in bringing the reality of his reign into the world—and into Tom's life.

Moving toward Application with Natalie

How does the theme of this passage minister to Natalie? We have seen that Natalie is a woman who truly seeks to live within God's redemptive plotline, but she has become weary in well-doing. How does Mark 1:40–45 give her a "gospel gaze" on her life, a wise perspective that shapes her thoughts, emotions, and actions, and invites her to deeper relationship with God?

The first thing I would like Natalie to notice from the passage is that the restoration Jesus brings is holistic—physical, spiritual, and social. It is true that sin (always in a global and sometimes in a specific sense) leads to spiritual, physical, and social "dislocation." But the coming of the kingdom brings restoration and *shalom* "far as the curse is found." How might this be helpful for Natalie to see?

> C: I want to spend some time interacting over the passage I asked you to read last week—Mark 1:40–45. Did you have time to do that?
>
> N: Yes, I spent some time prayerfully going through that passage and really, all of Mark 1.
>
> C: What did you notice about the kind of ministry Jesus carried out?

N: Well, it's full-orbed. Mark records healing, exorcism, teaching with authority, preaching, repentance, belief in the good news, and the calling of the disciples.

C: Yes. You see the physical, spiritual, and social impact of the kingdom. Is Jesus' ministry to the leper holistic also?

N: Definitely physical. Leprosy was a bodily condition, and Jesus healed him. Spiritual? Hmm. That seems less clear. It's interesting that Jesus didn't ask the leper to repent of any sin. Jesus *did* ask him to go to the priests to perform the sacrifices required as a result of his cleansing.

C: Yes—guilt and sin offerings were required for the one who had been pronounced clean by the priest (Lev. 14:12, 19). What does that suggest about the true nature of uncleanness due to leprosy (or anything else that made a person unclean)?

N: That uncleanness was more than skin deep! Physical uncleanness was associated with spiritual uncleanness. Uncleanness was evidence that restoration was needed between the person and God.

C: Right. OK, so you've touched on physical and spiritual. How about social?

N: Definitely. Lepers in both the Old Testament and New Testament were outcasts who had to live separately from others. So Jesus' cleansing of the leper would mean he could be reinstated to community life.

C: Great. Have you considered how your work is similar to Jesus' ministry?

N: Well, I can't say I've cured any cases of leprosy lately! [Smiles] I definitely have a holistic approach. I'm concerned about all aspects of my patients' lives—physical, spiritual, and social.

C: Do you see how your work is a critical part of God's holistic restoration of his creation?

N: I think I started my practice with that realization. One of the main reasons I wanted to do inner-city medicine was because I believed that gospel ministry involves word *and* deed. I don't know; maybe I've been a bit envious of my brother's and sister's "word" ministry and forgotten that

I really am participating in Jesus' kingdom-building work, even if it's a day when I mostly see folks with ear infections and sore throats![25]

C: That's true. Jesus moved toward the weak, the broken, the notorious sinners, the lame, the blind, and the sick. You have that same privilege, Natalie. I realize that this doesn't fully answer all your vocational questions. But I hope it brings needed perspective in the midst of your work now.

N: I think I'll spend some more time thinking about how my work ties in with Jesus' mission.

C: Great! No doubt, Mark wrote his Gospel because there remained (and remains) sin, illness, brokenness, relational alienation—all the facets of *"anti-shalom"* in the world. I'll be praying this week that you would be encouraged by the fact that you live on the front lines of God's kingdom mission. You colabor with Jesus!

Even with this perspective Natalie may still lament, "What impact am I having?" This may have crossed Jesus' mind as well, given the leper's disobedience and the subsequent hardships that resulted for Jesus. Remember, one reason for Jesus' command to silence was to guard against wrong expectations for what the promised reign of God would look like. Mark goes on to show that even the men Jesus invested in daily for three years didn't fully understand what he was doing, not even *after* the resurrection! (See Acts 1:6.) From an earthly perspective, Jesus' mission looked a colossal failure at the time of the crucifixion. Where were his followers? Where were the people he had healed and taught? Where was his inner circle? Only the resurrection and the outpouring of the Holy Spirit put things in rightful perspective.

The experience of resurrection *for us* is a certain but *future* hope. Think about this: the leper was healed but he ultimately died. The King touched his life, but death still awaited him. And we still live, as did Mark, in that tension of the times between the resurrection of Jesus and his return to consummate the kingdom. This means that, realistically, "impact" will often look far less than we desire. This, too, may help Natalie to persevere when she wonders what good she is doing.

Having a realistic picture of the already/not yet kingdom may also address vestiges of perfectionism in Natalie's life. Perfectionism is about control, overresponsibility, self-sufficiency, and achieving glory now. Natalie might have felt she was able to do that earlier, when life was less complex. Now the challenges she faces in practice are too much for even the most gifted of people. But God is gracious to bring us to the end of ourselves and our resources (as uncomfortable as that is!) because in those moments of inadequacy and insufficiency we taste the resurrection power of Jesus (2 Cor. 1:8–9). This does not mean that Natalie shouldn't weep when her hard work runs aground. But it does mean that her identity and worth are not tied up in her performance as a Christian physician.

As the passage hints (and the remainder of Mark's Gospel fully discloses), kingdom ministry does come with a cost—for Jesus *and* his followers. Perhaps Natalie wonders if full-time Christian ministry might feel more fulfilling. But it, too, is often fraught with costly self-sacrifice, imploding lives, and doubts about impact. The grass is not necessarily greener elsewhere! It's just a different lawn. And you still have to mow the lawn wherever you are! The writer of Hebrews exhorts the followers of Christ: "And so Jesus also suffered outside the city gate to make the people holy through his own blood. Let us, then, go to him outside the camp, bearing the disgrace he bore. For here we do not have an enduring city, but we are looking for the city that is to come" (13:12–14). Kingdom living is costly living, no matter where you serve.

Lastly, I believe the passage helps Natalie in the midst of her growing "compassion fatigue." The Gospel of Mark takes us on a breakneck pace. His first chapter has a particularly frenetic feel to it, as Jesus engages person after person, ministry situation after ministry situation. And yet what is Jesus' response to the lowly leper's request? "I am willing." Natalie's willingness and efforts (ability) to heal within medicine must not come in her own strength but in the willingness and power of Christ. Urge her to remember daily, "I can do everything through him who gives me strength" (Phil. 4:13). And the One who gives her strength is not some generic Jesus but a flesh-and-blood King, the crucified and risen Son of God, who indwells her through his Spirit.

Connecting Mark 1 to Natalie's life does not give her a prescription for a specific gospel-oriented obedience. The passage does not generate a single "You must do _____" kind of application. (You have seen how the passage may lead to different connections and applications for two different people.) But it should give Natalie perspective to make wise decisions about whether her situation warrants change. And it should shape her attitude even as she weighs a potential move. She may choose to leave her practice, but if she does, she will not be running away from the challenge. It will be with the conviction that God is calling her to other kingdom work. Finally, notice that I am not using Mark 1 to address *all* the aspects of her experience as a saint, sufferer, and sinner. No single passage will speak to all aspects of a person's struggles.

Conclusion

My hope is that these two chapters have given you a practical feel for connecting very different parts of Scripture with two very different people. I have shown just two of many ways to encourage the dialogue between God and a struggling person, which should lead to greater depth in relationship with God and others. I suspect, however, that you may still have questions about (or even objections to!) this redemptive-historical application in actual practice. Answering some of these questions is the focus of our final chapter.

Discussion Questions

1. Think of someone you are ministering to. (It can be the same person you considered in the previous chapter.) How might you use Mark 1:40–45 to minister to him or her?
2. What passage or passages in the New Testament have recently captured *your* attention? How would you use one of them to minister to Tom and Natalie? How about the person in question 1?

3. Consider the most recent New Testament passage you have read. Spend ten minutes prayerfully considering how you would use it in the life of the person from question 1. Now spend several hours this week doing some further study on the passage. How might this study amplify your use of this text with the same person?
4. As you near the end of this book, what questions do you have about the task of connecting Scripture to real life?

CHAPTER 11

Niagara Falls or a Cup of Cold Water in Jesus' Name?

You may be thinking at this point, *Thank you for complicating my ministry life! Using the Bible was simple until you came along!* Believe me, I've been there! I, too, continue to learn and grow in connecting Scripture with life. I have tried throughout this book to anticipate and address concerns you may have, but I realize that you still may have questions about the process of connecting Scripture to life in a redemptive-historical way. Let me use this chapter to pull the threads together and address the following statements and questions more fully:

- I still wonder whether the preparation required is too labor intensive. If I "stretch out the accordion" on a regular basis, whether it's analyzing the person or the text, I'll end up ministering to a maximum of one person a week (if I'm lucky)!
- What you propose is too involved, especially for people who don't have much familiarity with the Bible. It is not realistic for face-to-face ministry. Tom and Natalie were model counselees! I see the benefit of tying together the original context of a passage with the Bible as a whole

in preaching or teaching, but I don't think it's feasible in counseling or discipling.

- Do you *have* to open to a specific Bible passage when ministering the Word in a personal relationship? Are there other ways to help people connect their stories with the story of Scripture?

- Do you *have* to make an explicit connection to the gospel in every ministry encounter that uses Scripture?

- Or, put another way, can you really balance the details of a text with the overarching gospel-centered focus? At the end of the day, don't you risk submerging the details of a particular passage into the broader story line of Scripture? Doesn't the text become a mere springboard to other passages or to biblical "generalities"?[1]

- What about the Spirit in all of this? I'm worried that your method overshadows his work in the moment. It feels too mechanical.

- Your approach seems too individualistic. It doesn't take seriously the corporate context of spiritual growth, especially the local church. It also doesn't stress that God is in the process of transforming communities, societal structures, and culture—even the whole world!

I take these concerns seriously, and I have hope that by the end of this chapter I will have given several good answers. Because the questions include a lot of overlap, I'm not going to tackle them one by one. I'll take a more topical approach.

The Use of Scripture Is a Process, Not a One-Time Event

First, think of the use of Scripture in personal ministry as a process, not a one-time event. Ministry occurs over time! Tom and Natalie's stories were compressed for the sake of illustration, and because of that they can only go so far in depicting a live-action ministry encounter using the Word. Personal ministry, whether it involves counseling, mentoring, or discipling, is a dialogue, and that conversation occurs over time.[2]

Our goal is never to do a redemptive-historical "brain dump" into someone's life! Our goal is not to drown someone under the Niagara Falls of biblical truth but to give a cup of living water that will help sustain a person *today*. We need wisdom from God to know what is most needful for a particular point in time. One of my seminary professors once talked about the task of preaching by saying, "Don't bring the kitchen into the dining room. The kitchen is for preparation and the dining room is where you present and serve the food." In preaching we distill the fruits of our studies, tailoring our messages to meet the needs of our congregations. In a similar way in a discipling or counseling encounter, our thoughts about the person and about particular passages may well go beyond what we actually talk about when we're together. Remember, the ultimate goal is not to transmit huge amounts of information but to help a person meet with God through his Word!

Further, a spiral of understanding occurs as we continue to study Scripture and seek to understand particular people.[3] Our preconceived notions about how a text might relate to someone may well fall flat in practice. This sets us up for new opportunities to more deeply "read" the person and more deeply consider how the story of Scripture might connect with him or her.

I like the phrase that the Narnians use with one another near the end of C. S. Lewis' *The Last Battle,* the final book in *The Chronicles of Narnia.* As they enter a renewed Narnia and travel to their final home with Aslan, they encourage one another with the phrase, "Further up and further in!"[4] They can never plumb the depths of their experience: the further they go, the better and more expansive Aslan's country gets. In a similar way, our use of Scripture is a progressive journey in which we travel "further up and further in" in our understanding of people and texts. What we should experience is gospel-oriented, scripturally rooted conversation that produces fruit over time, not a stilted, one-time "data-dump" into someone's life.

It is true that we may only have the opportunity to meet once with a particular person. Although I am focused on longer-term counseling and discipling relationships in this book, which invite multiple connections between life and Scripture, God also gives us brief gospel conversations. In those situations we should seek to ask good questions, listen well, and consider what "bite-sized" aspect of the biblical story might be most helpful now, whether we open to chapter and verse or not. Keeping the approach of this book in mind, even for brief ministry encounters, should keep our conversations heart-oriented and Christ-centered.

Ongoing Relationship Is the Context for Ministry

In some ways this is evident in the preceding point, but I want to focus next on the relational context for connecting life and Scripture, which includes several aspects.

First, because we have an ongoing relationship with the persons we are counseling or discipling, maintaining a gospel or kingdom focus involves more than specific appeals to the Bible's overall redemptive plotline. An ongoing relationship with multiple conversations over time provides a natural framework in which specific scripturally rooted encounters find their place. We don't start the building from scratch every time we meet with people! Think of it like this: I don't awaken every morning and rehearse the "meta-narrative" of my courtship and marriage-to-date with my wife Jody in order to prepare for a more specific discussion of something such as finances. No, our shared experience lays the groundwork for diving right in to the issue at hand.

In a similar way, sharing Scripture with others is embedded in the ongoing "narrative" of the relationships with those persons—how we've incarnated the character of Christ, how we've rejoiced or wept with them over God's purposes in their lives, what we've previously talked about, what passages we've already discussed, and what we've experienced together. If the broader context of our ministry to these individuals is clearly and consistently grace-based and kingdom-centered, if the glory and wonder of the triune God's redemption is both in the background and in the forefront of what we say and do, then a specific appeal to redemptive-historical connections is not mandated every time we use Scripture. (But as we'll see below, such a kingdom-centered, Christ-focused appeal is not as time-consuming as you might think!)

Second, the very way we share Scripture with people is a part of what it means to love our neighbors well. In other words, the *process* of using Scripture in ministry is just as important as the *content* we hope the persons will grasp. Our use of Scripture should encourage conversation and promote relationship even when we are challenging others. It should meet people where they are living and not feel like a "bait-and-switch." Using Scripture should not feel like an awkward insertion into the conversation but a further exploration of the issue at hand. If you're met with blank stares and glazed eyes when you open your Bible, ask yourself why. It may have to do with *how* you do it more than the actual content you share. It's worth mentioning again that an extended mini-sermon is unlikely to be loving or wise!

We *Can* Focus on the Tip of the Iceberg

These first two points suggest that when we use Scripture with someone, we may touch on the tip of the iceberg (that is, focus on a specific action the passage suggests or tap into certain emotions the passage might evoke) without boring into the deeper redemptive-historical connections *at that point*. Here are two examples to explain what I mean.

A few months ago I was having a difficult time getting my daughter down for bed. She was balking about staying in her room, and she was on the edge of losing all control. I could feel my frustration level rise. Not only was my downtime being eaten up, but also I know the effects of insufficient sleep on my children—and it's not pretty. So I was quite invested in having my daughter go to bed in a timely way. (Although I must confess, I wasn't being very self-reflective or heart-focused at that point in time!) God, in his mercy, brought to mind something I had read earlier that day in Romans, specifically 12:21: "Do not be overcome by evil, but overcome evil with good." The call to me was clear: I needed to respond in a gracious manner, without impatience or harshness, and seek to be an instrument of true help to my daughter in her sleep struggle.

Now think about this. This was quite a specific, principle-oriented response, almost a "direct" line of application from the text to my life. I wasn't considering the surrounding verses or the purpose for which Paul wrote the book of Romans or how Jesus fit into that scheme. I appeared to be breaking all my own rules! And yet it was, I think, an appropriate application, and this was borne out with further reflection.[5]

I continued to chew on that verse in its larger context for the next few days. And I was struck with how Jesus himself exemplified overcoming evil with good. This led to connections with 1 Peter 2:22–23: "'He committed no sin, and no deceit was found in his mouth.' When they hurled their insults at him, he did not retaliate; when he suffered, he made no threats. Instead, he entrusted himself to him who judges justly." Who would have thought a nighttime encounter between a father and a daughter was a mini-drama meant to exhibit the character of Jesus on the cross?! Ultimately, it's not about me gritting my teeth to overcome evil with good. This is no arbitrary directive Paul gives in Romans! The real grounding for this command is the self-sacrificial heart of the gospel. But these realizations were not "front-loaded" into my initial response to my daughter. Rather, my personal application of Romans 12:21 expanded over time.

Here's a second example. In counseling I recently used 2 Corinthians 1:8–9 with a woman who has persevered and grown in the midst of chronic physical suffering but who has lately become more discouraged. Paul tells the Corinthians, "We do not want you to be uninformed, brothers, about the hardships we suffered in the province of Asia. We were under great pressure, far beyond our own ability to endure, so that we despaired even of life. Indeed, in our hearts we felt the sentence of death. But this happened that we might not rely on ourselves but on God, who raises the dead." That is exactly what was occurring in my counselee's life. She was learning to lean harder and harder on the resurrection power of Jesus in the midst of her pain. That's why I used the passage—to highlight that her life was a living example of what Paul was saying. It involved five minutes of conversation, and I believe it was encouraging to her; but again, I did not make explicit connections with the broader context of Corinthians or with other places in Scripture.[6]

That same kind of focused connection between the details of a passage and the details of someone's life also happened in Tom and Natalie's case studies. For example, I encouraged Tom to run to Jesus with the same desperate dependence that the leper did in Mark 1:40–45, rather than sit in a place of discouragement or self-pity. It's very possible that in a real-time counseling session such an emphasis would make up most of the conversation. It might include issues such as Tom's perceived barriers to drawing near to Jesus, the cost of not coming, and the places other than Jesus Tom might be tempted to run.

Let me change from the iceberg metaphor and suggest that you view the passage as an onion with multiple layers of truth and perspective. Sometimes you will find it appropriate to deal with only one aspect (one layer) of a passage, as you discern which aspect(s) of a person's life are most critical to address in the moment. The realities of living as a saint, sufferer, and sinner suggest a multiplicity of "life layers" to explore together. So, while it's true that the gospel is first and foremost the good news about Jesus Christ before it is good news for us,[7] the process in practice doesn't always move linearly from original context to redemptive-historical context to our own personal context, especially in an unscripted encounter.

But (and this is a huge "but" on which the premise of the book rests!) if in my use of Scripture with others I'm *consistently* overlooking the original context *and/or* the connections to God's redemption in Christ, then I have ignored the redemptive-historical character of the Bible. I miss the fact that God acts and reveals himself in time and space, climaxing in Christ's death and resurrection and the outpouring of the Spirit for the church. As a result, I miss that my obedience to Scripture occurs in the overlap between "this age" and the "age to come" and that I am among those "on whom the fulfillment of the ages has come" (1 Cor. 10:11).[8] I miss the fact that redemption has an already-and-not-yet aspect to it—God's redemption, his new creation, his kingdom have already broken into the world through Jesus Christ but are not yet fully realized and completed until Jesus returns.[9] As a result, I may move toward unrealistic optimism (an exclusive focus on the already) or pessimism (an exclusive focus on the not yet) as I minister to others. Further, I risk giving directives and suggesting applications without providing the gospel foundation for such counsel.

Thus, it may be helpful to focus on "the tip of the iceberg" when we use Scripture in a particular ministry encounter. But if our approach to the Bible is consistently fragmented and piecemeal, it cannot bring gospel-centered perspectives to the complex facets of a person's life. These redemptive perspectives are what invite a person into a deeper, transforming relationship with God.

Clearly, the longer we sit with a passage (and a person!) the more we see, and the richer the gospel connections between life and Scripture. Often in my counseling I will have a person "camp out" in a particular passage for several weeks at time. Inhabiting a passage like this helps people make it their own and fosters the kinds of connections this book has suggested.

It May Only Take a Minute (or Less!)

At the same time, it doesn't necessarily take hours of study and face-to-face time to make redemptive-historical, kingdom-centered connections for people.

Recently during a counseling session, I referred to Exodus 16 (God's provision of manna) as a way to support the biblical truths that God's grace is sufficient for the day and that you can't "hoard" grace in advance.[10] God gives us what we need for the day at hand. I could have connected it more clearly with Jesus, the Bread of Life (John 6), with only a few additional comments. Why didn't I? I reflected on it later and realized that it was a case of simple omission in the moment. I hadn't planned ahead of time to use the Exodus passage—it came to mind during the session. A helpful point might have been further strengthened if I had made that more personal connection to Jesus.

Similarly, consider again my earlier example of using 2 Corinthians 1:8–9 in ministry to a suffering counselee. It would have been appropriate in another conversation to make connections to verses 3–4, which relate Paul's (and our) experience of suffering to the sufferings of Christ. It also would provide a jumping-off point to talk about interdependence within the body of Christ in the context of suffering. In this case, the omission was more "strategic"—I simply wanted to tie together Paul's experience of tasting the resurrection power of Jesus in the midst of hardship with my counselee's own experience.

But, clearly, we *can* make specific redemptive-historical or Christ-centered connections without an extensive journey through Scripture or an intensive review of the Bible's unified story.

Notice that the biblical writers do the same thing, even in the midst of passages that have a more dominant "imperative" character. Take Ephesians 4:29–32, for example:

> Do not let any unwholesome talk come out of your mouths, but only what is helpful for building others up according to their needs, that it may benefit those who listen. And do not grieve the Holy Spirit of God, with whom you were sealed for the day of redemption. Get rid of all bitterness, rage and anger, brawling and slander, along with every form of malice. Be kind and compassionate to one another, forgiving each other, just as in Christ God forgave you.

This is a command-laden portion of Scripture. Paul does not stop midstream and say to the Ephesians, "By the way, this command is grounded in the realities of redemption that I outlined in chapter 1. Go back and reread that section before you try to obey these commands." What he does do is make several comments, almost in passing, that put a redemptive spin on the commands. He mentions the Holy Spirit, "with whom you were sealed for the day of redemption," and uses the phrase "just as in Christ God forgave you."

Similarly, when we use Scripture, it may not take much to move from the particulars of a passage to their Christological significance, applied to the person's life. The more we immerse ourselves in Scripture and the more self-conscious we are in our approach to people, the more natural and spontaneous these connections will be.

Wisdom in Action, Not Regurgitated Rules

"You didn't do much of anything you taught us to do!" This is a frequent comment from students in my counseling observation class. These students have taken several introductory counseling courses that lay out a basic framework for counseling, but the observation class is the first time many have seen the concepts and proposed methodology "live and in color." They're running up against the fact that real-life ministry requires wise creativity and Spirit-dependent flexibility, not slavish adherence to a set of rules.

It's not that a structured framework isn't important, but a natural progression occurs as we learn and grow in a particular skill set. When I have the opportunity, I like to create pottery on the wheel. This involves wedging a lump of clay, centering it on the wheel, opening the centered mound of clay, raising the wall, shaping the pot, and adding finishing touches. At first, I closely and self-consciously followed the steps my first instructor taught me. Over time, I have incorporated the techniques of other teachers and have begun to develop a style of my own. Although the basic progression of steps remains the same—I ignore the basic framework to my own peril!—I now move with greater ease and spontaneity, much less conscious of the individual steps I am taking.

My hope is that you will view this book as providing helpful guidelines for connecting Scripture with life in a gospel-centered way—but not as a strict "formula" and not in isolation from the insights of others who have tackled the challenge of application in some way. As you wisely listen to and interpret both people and texts over time, you will find that the approach is not as labor intensive as you might think, and you will find that connecting Scripture to life in Christ-centered, meaningful ways happens more and more naturally.[11]

Spirit-Dependent Connections

Fruitful application doesn't always require a long process of Bible study or prayerful meditation, as the examples in this chapter have illustrated. Similarly, you may be able speak a "word in season" to someone even before you know her very well. Of course, everything I've said in this book moves in the direction of a deeper engagement with the Scriptures and with people. But lest we think we can "master" an approach to Scripture or to people, we need to remember that it is ultimately God's Spirit who uses his Word to transform us into the image of Christ. Often it is the spontaneous passing comment that the Spirit uses in someone's life, not what *I* had thought would be the connecting point between the person and Scripture. How humbling— and how appropriate!

Because of the Spirit's presence and work, we can be confident that as "the rain and the snow come down from heaven, and do not return to it without watering the earth and making it bud and flourish, so that it yields seed for the sower and bread for the eater, so is my word that goes out from my mouth: It will not return to me empty, but will accomplish what I desire and achieve the purpose for which I sent it" (Isa. 55:10–11).

Growth Happens in Community

The emphasis of this book has been to highlight how you as an individual can bring the riches of God's redemptive story to bear on another's life. But it is important to remember that transformation into the character of Christ and alignment with his mission for renewing the whole world occur within the church community (Eph. 4:1–16). As the title of Tod Bolsinger's book declares, *It Takes a Church to Raise a Christian.*[12]

Living into God's story doesn't simply take place in my private devotions or when another believer speaks a timely word of truth and I take it to heart. These *are* important contexts for growth, but we also grab hold of a kingdom vision for life in the context of community gatherings, particularly worship. As a result of gathering for worship, confessing our sin, hearing the Word, praying as a body, and receiving the sacraments, we are strengthened in our faith to go forth and serve God and others.[13] As saints we are reminded of our identity and purpose in Christ. As sufferers we find comfort in the good news that Jesus has overcome evil and will return. As sinners we are challenged to repent and to align our lives with gospel values. What happens within the gathered community should fuel one-on-one ministry opportunities throughout the week, just as our own devotional intake of Scripture does.

175

Connecting Scripture with Life Happens in Many Ways

In light of what I have been saying so far, you would be right to conclude that there are many "modes" of ministering the Word—some more planned and proactive, others more spontaneous—as we remain dependent on the Spirit in the ministry moment.[14] What might this look like in personal ministry? Here are some examples.

- Mention a biblical theme or truth without necessarily quoting chapter and verse. For example, "God cares about the unjust things that have happened to you." Or, "As a believer you have a new identity in Jesus Christ, not an identity dictated by the opinions of others." Or, "Your first priority is to honor Christ, not necessarily to please your demanding friend." As you grow in biblical wisdom, there will be an increasing overlap between your words and God's Word. Not that your words have authority and power in and of themselves! Rather, as your own life is increasingly conformed to the character of Christ, your speech will manifest the wisdom of Jesus, even if you don't open the Bible to a particular passage in conversation with someone else.

- Open to a passage that you think may connect with the person's experience, and use it as a stimulus for conversation. Certainly I leaned in that direction when presenting the model and when I discussed how Haggai 2 and Mark 1 might connect with Tom and Natalie. As I mentioned above, sometimes this conversation touches on the tip of the iceberg for a few minutes. At other times it is more comprehensive, incorporating details of the original context and the passage's fulfillment in the coming of Jesus as the springboard for application.

- Ask people what passages have been most meaningful to them recently. Have them describe how they have been helped. This gives you a natural point of connection between their lives and Scripture and you can build on that foundation. It also gives you a sense of the person's intake and application of Scripture.

- If ministering more formally (for example, in weekly counseling or discipleship/mentoring appointments), give a passage as homework to discuss at the next session. Often I will suggest some specific questions to consider. They pave the way for making connections with the person's life.

- Camp out in a passage or book for several weeks or longer with the person. As I mentioned earlier, this allows you to explore many aspects of the passage over time. It helps people to see the issues of their lives in light of the ways the passage speaks to them as saints, sufferers, and sinners.

- Pray through a particular passage together. Alternatively, have the person write a prayer that expresses the details and themes of the text.

- Listen to a song or hymn that captures certain biblical themes or is based upon a specific passage. Several years ago, I opened a counseling session by playing the hymn "Come Ye Sinners, Poor and Wretched," wanting my counselee to taste the freedom that comes from full forgiveness in Jesus. Little did I know that he would come to the session greatly burdened by a recent sin. The song moved him and provided the impetus he needed to confess his sin right then and there. I'm not certain that talking about his sin or the need for forgiveness or even opening to a passage like 1 John 1:9 would have prompted the same response.

- Listen to a sermon or teaching and discuss how it specifically applies to the person you are serving. (And don't forget to talk about how it applies to you too!)

In every case, you want to consider your pastoral purpose for sharing the Scripture. In other words, have you considered your goal for using Scripture, particularly if you are planning to use a particular text? Are you intending to comfort, warn, encourage, convict, give hope, challenge, deepen joy, resolve confusion, calm fear, or prompt specific action (among many other goals)?[15] Too often, we don't consider our purpose in bringing biblical truth to bear upon a person's life. We don't consider, based on our knowledge of the person and Scripture, what is most needed in the moment. And so our use of Scripture can have a "shotgun" feel to it, rather than a Spirit-directed application that meets the need of the hour.

Odysseus vs. Jason and Orpheus

An example from Greek mythology can serve as a closing parable about what I hope and pray our use of Scripture will be like.[16]

Homer tells the story of Odysseus who, in his travels, had to sail past the Sirens, Greek nymphs whose beautiful singing would lure sailors to their deaths on the rocks. Odysseus knew the danger, but he was also curious to hear the Sirens' song. He had all his sailors plug up their ears with beeswax so they couldn't hear the seductive music. But Odysseus had himself tied to the mast, leaving his own ears unplugged. He ordered his men to leave him tied to the mast no matter how much he begged to be freed. And, of course, they did proceed safely though Odysseus strained against the ropes that bound him until they were past.

Another story from Greek mythology has Jason and his companions sailing past the Sirens as well. But in this story, rather than a defensive maneuver, Jason had Orpheus play his lyre as they neared the islands of the Sirens. The beautiful melody Orpheus played drowned out the Sirens' song, with the result that they sailed safely past.

Too often our attempts to connect Scripture with life leave people in the position of Odysseus, unchanged and still pining for the siren song of the world, the flesh, and the devil. I'm convinced that, in large measure, it is because we have ignored the redemptive-historical character of God's story and the narrative structure of people's lives as saints, sufferers, and sinners. As a result, our use of Scripture never really connects the heart of people's struggles with the glorious, unfolding story of redemption that climaxes in the coming of Jesus. Details of the Bible remain disconnected from the details of people's lives when we overlook the redemptive meta-narrative that encompasses them both.

My hope in writing this book is that the music people would hear as we use the Scriptures would be a gospel-rich, kingdom-focused, Christ-centered symphony in their ears, with the result that the alternative (and ultimately false) voices and stories that beguile them are drowned out increasingly to insignificance. May you increasingly know the One to whom the story of Scripture points so that no matter where you are in the Bible, you may consistently help your fellow saints, sufferers, and sinners live out his powerful and redemptive message.

Discussion Questions

1. What other "modes" of ministering the Word have you used to help someone connect the riches of Scripture with the realities of life?
2. Is your use of the Bible in personal ministry a "gospel symphony"? Why or why not?
3. How will your approach to people and Scripture change as a result of reading this book?
4. What questions still remain as you consider this approach to Scripture and to people?

Summary of Questions from Chapter 7

Questions to Help You Understand the Person

1. *Saint*
   a. What evidence of God's grace do you see in the person's life?
   b. In what ways do you see the individual already living true to his identity in Christ? (How does the person already exhibit the character of Christ in word and deed?)
2. *Sufferer*
   a. What situational stressors is the person facing? (Consider physical, relational, circumstantial, and social/cultural issues.)
   b. What were the significant shaping events of his life?
   c. How has he been sinned against?
   d. How is the person experiencing his problems?
3. *Sinner*
   a. What desires, thoughts, emotions, and actions are out of line with gospel/kingdom values?
   b. What motives, themes, and interpretations of life "compete" with the biblical story?

Questions to Help You Understand the Passage

1. *Original Context*
   a. What has happened in redemptive history up to the time the passage/book was written?
   b. Based upon careful study of the historical, grammatical, and literary features of the passage, what do you think God and the human author were communicating to their audience at this particular point in redemptive history? What seems to be the main theme/point?
   c. What response do you think was intended? How might this message have affected the lives of the original audience?

2. *Expanded (Redemptive-Historical) Context*
   a. Why was this passage particularly important at the stage of redemptive history in which it was written?
   b. How is the main theme/thought of your passage present in earlier and later writings?
   c. In what ways is your passage an "unfinished" story?
   d. How do the themes of your passage connect with the life, death, and resurrection of Jesus Christ and with the church?

3. *Moving toward Application*
   a. How does this passage, in light of gospel connections (see 2d above), address people as saints, sufferers, and sinners?
      i.   What does this passage say about the identity and privilege of being part of God's people?
      ii. What does it say about the nature and purpose of suffering and how God approaches the sufferer?
      iii. What does the passage say or suggest about the conduct of God's people? How should the message of the passage shape the thoughts, attitudes, emotions, or actions of the person you serve?
   b. More broadly, how does this passage give the person you are helping a better "lens" to interpret his experiences? In view of that, how should he live before God and others?

Recommended Resources

For Reading Scripture as a Cohesive Story

- Craig G. Bartholomew and Michael W. Goheen, *The Drama of Scripture: Finding Our Place in the Biblical Story* (Grand Rapids, MI: Baker Academic, 2004).
- Mark Strom, *The Symphony of Scripture: Making Sense of the Bible's Many Themes* (Phillipsburg, NJ: P & R, 2001).

For Instruction on How to Interpret the Bible

- Jeannine K. Brown, *Scripture as Communication: Introducing Biblical Hermeneutics* (Grand Rapids, MI: Baker Academic, 2007).
- Tremper Longman III, *Reading the Bible with Heart and Mind* (Colorado Springs, CO: NavPress, 1997).
- Dan McCartney and Charles Clayton, *Let the Reader Understand: A Guide to Interpreting and Applying the Bible,* 2nd ed. (Phillipsburg, NJ: P & R, 2002).

For Doing Additional Biblical Study

- D. A. Carson and Douglas J. Moo, *An Introduction to the New Testament,* 2nd ed. (Grand Rapids, MI: Zondervan, 2005).

- Tremper Longman III and Raymond B. Dillard, *An Intro-duction to the Old Testament,* 2nd ed. (Grand Rapids, MI: Zondervan, 2006).
- Leland Ryken, James C. Wilhoit, and Tremper Longman III, *Dictionary of Biblical Imagery* (Downers Grove, IL: InterVarsity Press, 1998).

For Personal Ministry (General Approach)

- Timothy S. Lane and Paul David Tripp, *How People Change,* 2nd ed. (Greensboro, NC: New Growth Press, 2008).
- Paul David Tripp, *Instruments in the Redeemer's Hands: People in Need of Change Helping People in Need of Change* (Phillipsburg, NJ: P & R, 2002).
- Leslie Vernick, *How to Live Right When Your Life Goes Wrong* (Colorado Springs, CO: Waterbrook Press, 2003).

The Web site of the Christian Counseling & Educational Foundation (CCEF) has a host of resources to help you address particular problems of life from a biblical perspective. You can access it at www.ccef.org.

Notes

Introduction

1. See Daniel M. Doriani, *Putting the Truth to Work: The Theory and Practice of Biblical Application* (Phillipsburg, NJ: P & R, 2001) and Bryan Chapell, *Christ-Centered Preaching: Redeeming the Expository Sermon,* 2nd ed. (Grand Rapids, MI: Baker Academic, 2005).

2. See Richard B. Hays, *The Moral Vision of the New Testament: Community, Cross, New Creation; A Contemporary Introduction to New Testament Ethics* (San Francisco: HarperCollins, 1996), Christopher J. H. Wright, *Old Testament Ethics for the People of God* (Downers Grove, IL: InterVarsity Press, 2004), and William J. Webb, *Slaves, Homosexuals, and Women: Exploring the Hermeneutics of Cultural Analysis* (Downers Grove, IL: InterVarsity Press, 2001) as examples.

3. A very helpful resource is Tremper Longman III, *Reading the Bible with Heart and Mind* (Colorado Springs, CO: NavPress, 1997).

4. For excellent overviews of this issue, see Dan McCartney and Charles Clayton, *Let the Reader Understand: A Guide to Interpreting and Applying the Bible,* 2nd ed. (Phillipsburg, NJ: P & R, 2002), 291–301, and also Jeannine K. Brown, *Scripture as Communication: Introducing Biblical Hermeneutics* (Grand Rapids, MI: Baker Academic, 2007), 19–136.

5. More comprehensive resources include Timothy S. Lane and Paul David Tripp, *How People Change,* 2nd ed. (Greensboro, NC: New Growth Press, 2008); Eric L. Johnson, *Foundations for Soul Care: A Christian Psychology Proposal* (Downers Grove, IL: InterVarsity Press, 2007); Paul David Tripp, *Instruments in the Redeemer's Hands: People in Need of Change Helping People in Need of Change* (Phillipsburg, NJ: P & R, 2002); Leslie Vernick, *How to Live Right When Your Life Goes Wrong* (Colorado Springs, CO: Waterbrook Press, 2003).

6. B. B. Warfield calls this "concursive operation." *The Inspiration and Authority of the Bible* (Phillipsburg, NJ: P & R, 1948), 95.

7. Brown, *Scripture as Communication,* 255ff. The term originates with Nicholas Wolterstorff, *Divine Discourse: Philosophical Reflections on the Claim That God Speaks* (Cambridge: Cambridge University Press, 1995).

8. For an excellent essay on reading the Bible as a cohesive narrative, see Richard Bauckham, "Reading Scripture as a Coherent Story" in *The Art of Reading Scripture,* eds. Ellen F. Davis and Richard B. Hays (Grand Rapids, MI: Eerdmans, 2003), 38–53. By the way, if you do not come from a theological tradition that highlights the continuity between God's dealings with humanity in the Old Testament and in the New Testament, you may not agree entirely with my view of the Scriptures. But I would encourage you to consider in a prayerful way the material that follows.

9. That is, God works out and explains his plan of redemption progressively over time.

10. Eugene Peterson, *Eat This Book: A Conversation in the Art of Spiritual Reading* (Grand Rapids, MI: Eerdmans, 2006), 20.

Chapter 1

1. Numbers 5:11–31 discusses the actions a husband should take if he suspects his wife of adultery. The process involves bringing his wife to the priest and having her drink a mixture of holy water and dust from the tabernacle floor. If she is guilty, the "bitter water" will result in a curse of bitter suffering. If she is innocent, the water will not harm her.

2. Peter Enns, *Exodus, The NIV Application Commentary* (Grand Rapids, MI: Zondervan, 2000), 30–31.

3. As we will see in later chapters, "relevance" lies at the junction of an understanding of the text and an understanding of the person. Often, when someone does not find a passage meaningful to his struggle, it means that you didn't properly understand the passage (and so forced a superficial relevance) or you didn't understand the particulars of the person's struggle (right-passage-wrong-person syndrome)—or both!

4. Not to mention the "religious" gap! What gives us the right to use *Israel's* Scriptures in our lives? We haven't really addressed that issue yet but will when we look at the nature of the Bible in chapter 3.

5. Of course, this claim needs scriptural support, which I will give in chapter 3.

6. Referencing Wolterstorff, Jeannine K. Brown, *Scripture as Communication: Introducing Biblical Hermeneutics* (Grand Rapids, MI: Baker Academic, 2007), 255.

Chapter 2

1. The first three of these approaches bear similarity to Richard Hays's "modes of appeal to Scripture" as rules, principles, and paradigms (Richard B. Hays, *The Moral Vision of the New Testament: Community, Cross, New Creation; A Contemporary Introduction to New Testament Ethics* [San Francisco: HarperCollins, 1996], 208–209).

2. In reality this question has to be addressed even when viewing the Bible as the story of God's redemptive work climaxing in Messiah Jesus. But as we will see, viewing the Scriptures in this "narratival" way provides a better pathway to discern how ancient commands and prohibitions apply today.

3. William J. Webb introduces *Slaves, Homosexuals, and Women* with a similar exercise (Downers Grove, IL: InterVarsity Press, 2001), 13–16.

4. See Exodus 20:2, which introduces the Ten Commandments and places them in a particular context: "I am the LORD your God, who brought you out of Egypt, out of the land of slavery." Peter Enns brings out the challenge of applying the Ten Commandments today in *Exodus, The NIV Application Commentary* (Grand Rapids, MI: Zondervan, 2000), 409–33.

5. Often this dilemma is solved by blending this "rule" approach with a view of Scripture as providing general principles, which will be discussed next. That is, the "kernel of truth" from a specific, historically situated command is taken as a general principle to be applied in the modern day. So, "Greet one another with a holy kiss" (1 Cor. 16:20b) may not be applied literally but rather distilled to the principle "Warmly greet one another in the Lord." The specific application of that principle may be a handshake, a hug, a smile, or a bob of the head. See Jeannine K. Brown, *Scripture as Communication: Introducing Biblical Hermeneutics* (Grand Rapids, MI: Baker Academic, 2007), 269–70.

6. From a Reformed perspective you might say that covenant precedes command. Relationship initiated by God precedes rules.

7. If you are struggling with an addiction to crack cocaine and can't pay the electric bill, where should you turn in Scripture?! To use language from the last chapter, the Bible may end up being reduced to ditch passages that yield either specific instruction or general principles, primarily for ditch problems.

8. L. Gregory Jones, "Embodying Scripture in the Community of Faith," in *The Art of Reading Scripture,* eds. Ellen F. Davis and Richard B. Hays (Grand Rapids, MI: Eerdmans, 2003), 147.

9. As we will see in the next chapter, the New Testament writers embed ethical instruction—including rules, norms, and principles—in a broader redemptive-historical framework. That framework, centering

on the climax of redemption in Christ, is sometimes stated, but it is always at least understood. The cross and resurrection are always the "home base" to which the New Testament writers appeal, explicitly or implicitly.

10. However, the writer of Samuel doesn't ignore David's potentially violent temper in the account of Nabal and Abigail (1 Sam. 25). In this account, Abigail's virtue and wisdom are highlighted in contrast to Nabal *and* David. See Jayne V. Clark, "Confronted by Anger," *Journal of Biblical Counseling* 24, no. 1 (Winter 2006): 6–13. And then, of course, there is the matter of David and Bathsheba (2 Sam. 11—12). This reminds us that we can't unequivocally appeal to biblical characters, as most are portrayed with both virtues and vices. In this way the biblical characters are surely like us!

11. J. Wilbur Chapman, "Jesus! What a Friend for Sinners!" 1910. *Trinity Hymnal,* rev. ed. (Norcross, GA: Great Commission Publications, 1990), hymn 498.

12. For example, the Council of Nicea (325) condemned the Christology of Arius and instead affirmed that the Son was "coequal, consubstantial, and coeternal" with the Father. Their labors yielded the Nicene Creed, perhaps the shortest of "systematic" theologies!

13. The traditional divisions of systematic theology include Scripture, Nature of God, Nature of Mankind, Christ's Person and Work, Salvation, the Church, and Last Things.

14. Of course, this is not necessarily a bad thing. We all come to Scripture with certain expectations and presuppositions based on our theological heritage, our experiences, our current relationships, and so on. The issue is not *do* we have presuppositions? Rather, do we *know* what they are and how they might affect our interpretive process? My theological "grid" for approaching Scripture is from a Reformed (Calvinistic) perspective, and I would support the view that the Westminster Confession of Faith accurately represents the doctrinal content of the Bible. Although these assumptions shape my approach to Scripture, they must not *prejudice* me from learning from other traditions. See Brown, *Scripture as Communication,* 120–36.

15. Systematic theologian Michael Williams is helpful here: "What is the Bible in such a system? It is a depository for proof-texts. A proof-text is a biblical statement or citation that [purportedly!] does not require a context in order to be coherent and meaningful. Its function has nothing to do with the over-arching biblical story in which it is embedded or in the specific genre in which it is found. Also, the function of a proof-text is assigned by an extra-biblical structure: the system of doctrine. The Bible exists primarily to support the system. . . ." Williams, "Systematic

Theology as a Biblical Discipline," 203, http://www.biblicaltheology.ca/blue_files/Systematic%20Theology.pdf (accessed Dec. 24, 2008).

16. Ibid., 209.

Chapter 3

1. Ben Witherington III, *Paul's Narrative Thought World: The Tapestry of Tragedy and Triumph* (Louisville, KY: Westminster/John Knox Press, 1994), 2.

2. See, for example, Brian J. Walsh and J. Richard Middleton, *The Transforming Vision: Shaping a Christian World View* (Downers Grove, IL: IVP, 1984) and Albert M. Wolters, *Creation Regained: Biblical Basis for a Reformational Worldview,* 2nd ed. (Grand Rapids, MI: Eerdmans, 2005).

3. Craig G. Bartholomew and Michael W. Goheen, *The Drama of Scripture: Finding Our Place in the Biblical Story* (Grand Rapids, MI: Baker Academic, 2004), 27.

4. Graeme Goldsworthy, *The Goldsworthy Trilogy: Gospel and Kingdom, Gospel and Wisdom, The Gospel in Revelation* (Carlisle, Cumbria: Paternoster Press, 2000), 54.

5. What follows is a brief overview of a rich and complex topic explored in much more depth in other sources. These include Bartholomew and Goheen, *The Drama of Scripture;* Edmund P. Clowney, *The Unfolding Mystery: Discovering Christ in the Old Testament* (Phillipsburg, NJ: P & R, 1988); O. Palmer Robertson, *The Christ of the Covenants* (Phillipsburg, NJ: P & R, 1980); Christopher J. H. Wright, *Knowing Jesus Through the Old Testament* (Downers Grove, IL: InterVarsity Press, 1992) and *The Mission of God: Unlocking the Bible's Grand Narrative* (Downers Grove, IL: IVP Academic, 2006); N. T. Wright, *The Climax of the Covenant: Christ and the Law in Pauline Theology* (Minneapolis, MN: Fortress, 1993) and *The Challenge of Jesus: Rediscovering Who Jesus Was and Is* (Downers Grove, IL: InterVarsity Press, 1999).

6. I am indebted to Douglas Green (Westminster Theological Seminary, Philadelphia) for this insight as part of his classroom exposition of Psalm 1.

7. N. T. Wright, *What St. Paul Really Said: Was Paul of Tarsus the Real Founder of Christianity?* (Grand Rapids, MI: Eerdmans, 1997), 127.

8. For an extended treatment of this theme, see Michael J. Gorman, *Cruciformity: Paul's Narrative Spirituality of the Cross* (Grand Rapids, MI: Eerdmans, 2001.)

9. See Dan G. McCartney, "The New Testament's Use of the Old Testament," in *Inerrancy and Hermeneutic,* ed. Harvie M. Conn (Grand Rapids, MI: Baker, 1988), 112–13.

10. Ibid., 113. He also notes 1 Peter 1:10–12, which provides the same interpretive framework as Luke 24.

11. Other sermons in Acts make similar connections between the Old Testament and the person and work of Jesus (e.g., Acts 2:14–36; 3:11–26).

12. I don't believe that this promise/fulfillment outline is restricted to specific instances of promise or prophecy although it includes those instances. Rather, the coming of Jesus fulfills everything in the Old Testament. The book of Hebrews makes this plain: the law, the sacrifices, the tabernacle, the very practices of Israelite worship were a shadow of the true realities to come in Christ.

13. Witherington, *Paul's Narrative Thought World*, 5.

14. Wright, *Knowing Jesus*, 8.

15. Witherington, *Paul's Narrative Thought World*, 5.

16. We looked at the importance of the context of a command in the last chapter. The context gives the relational rationale for the imperative.

17. David Powlison, "The Practical Theology of Counseling," *Journal of Biblical Counseling* 25, no. 2 (Spring 2007): 2. See also his article, "Counsel Ephesians," *Journal of Biblical Counseling* 17, no. 2 (Winter 1999): 2–11.

18. Jeannine Brown uses the term "(re)contextualization" instead of application to highlight the fact that the messages of the biblical writers were already contextualized (applied) to their original audiences (*Scripture as Communication: Introducing Biblical Hermeneutics* [Grand Rapids, MI: Baker Academic, 2007], 233).

19. Kathryn Tanner, "Scripture as Popular Text," *Modern Theology* 14, no. 2 (April 1998): 279–98.

Chapter 4

1. The Scripture Project, "Nine Theses on the Interpretation of Scripture" in *The Art of Reading Scripture*, eds. Ellen F. Davis and Richard B. Hays (Grand Rapids, MI: Eerdmans, 2003), 2.

2. David Steinmetz discusses this same reading strategy for the Bible using the detective genre in "Uncovering a Second Narrative: Detective Fiction and the Construction of Historical Method" in *The Art of Reading Scripture*, 54–68.

3. Two other movies with endings that force a total reorientation of understanding are *The Sixth Sense* and *The Fight Club*. Of course, even if the ending is not a huge surprise, you will view the film with the ending in mind as you watch it again.

4. Peter Enns, "Apostolic Hermeneutics and an Evangelical Doctrine of Scripture: Moving Beyond a Modernist Impasse," *Westminster Theological Journal* 65 (2003): 282.

5. I will talk in later chapters about how to combine a slow, savory approach to the Scriptures with the often fast-paced, unscripted aspects of personal ministry.

6. I realize that it's not always clear who the original readers were, but most introductions to the Old Testament and New Testament give this kind of background help for study.

7. For a comprehensive treatment of this theme, see Christopher J. H. Wright, *The Mission of God: Unlocking the Bible's Grand Narrative* (Downers Grove, IL: IVP Academic, 2006).

8. C. S. Lewis, *The Weight of Glory and Other Addresses* (New York: Touchstone/Simon & Schuster, 1996), 26.

9. C. S. Lewis, *The Voyage of the Dawn Treader: The Chronicles of Narnia, Book 5* (New York: HarperCollins, 1994), 213–14.

10. Eugene Peterson, *Eat This Book: A Conversation in the Art of Spiritual Reading* (Grand Rapids, MI: Eerdmans, 2006), 65.

11. You see the backward look in many psalms, notably 77, 78, 105, and 106, coupled with implications for the present worship of God. In the New Testament, 1 Peter 1:3–16 captures the interplay of past, present, and future aspects of God's redemption.

12. For a more in-depth treatment of this point, see Stephen E. Fowl and L. Gregory Jones, *Reading in Communion: Scripture and Ethics in Christian Life* (Eugene, OR: Wipf and Stock, 1998).

13. Craig G. Bartholomew and Michael W. Goheen, *The Drama of Scripture: Finding Our Place in the Biblical Story* (Grand Rapids, MI: Baker Academic, 2004), 12.

14. N. T. Wright, *The New Testament and the People of God* (Minneapolis, MN: Fortress Press, 1992), 40.

Chapter 5

1. One way to understand the experience of "midlife crisis" is as a midlife evaluation—and sometimes repudiation—of the dominant story (or stories) by which life had meaning and purpose up to that point.

2. Brian J. Walsh and J. Richard Middleton, *The Transforming Vision: Shaping a Christian World View* (Downers Grove, IL: IVP, 1984), 35. See also Christopher J. H. Wright, *The Mission of God: Unlocking the Bible's Grand Narrative* (Downers Grove, IL: IVP Academic, 2006), 55.

3. This is not to say that we can't have several stories vying for prominence at any given moment!

4. Joel B. Green, "The (Re-)Turn to Narrative" in *Narrative Reading, Narrative Preaching: Reuniting New Testament Interpretation and Proclamation,*

eds. Joel B. Green and Michael Pasquarello III (Grand Rapids, MI: Baker Academic, 2003), 17.

5. Of course, I'm referencing a story within a story: I'm focusing now on what God spoke to Adam and Eve directly (i.e., what Adam and Eve would have known) vs. the broader story of God's creation embedded in the book of Genesis, which was written to shape the worldview of God's people at a later point in history.

6. Bartholomew and Goheen note, "In God's kingdom, which he has set up by creating it, the special role he has assigned to humanity is that we should serve as his 'under-kings,' vice-regents, or stewards. We are to rule over the creation so that God's reputation is enhanced within his cosmic kingdom. . . . [W]e are God's royal stewards, put here to develop the hidden potential in God's creation so that the whole of it may celebrate his glory" (Craig G. Bartholomew and Michael W. Goheen, *The Drama of Scripture: Finding Our Place in the Biblical Story* [Grand Rapids, MI: Baker Academic, 2004], 37). For a full but more technical treatment of this idea, see Dan G. McCartney, "*Ecce Homo:* The Coming of the Kingdom as the Restoration of Human Vicegerency," *Westminster Theological Journal* 56 (1994): 1–21.

7. You can make the argument that the serpent lied on both accounts: death (spiritual and physical) entered the world *and* rather than becoming like God, knowing good and evil, they *lost* the ability to discern between good and evil. The downhill slide of humanity in the next chapters seems to confirm that interpretation. (Douglas Green, Unpublished Lecture Notes, Old Testament History and Theology 1, Westminster Theological Seminary, 1998.)

8. Of course, even in the consequences of the fall found in Genesis 3:14–19 you see glimmers of hope (in v. 15) that the disastrous, ongoing consequences were *not* the end of the story.

9. Richard A. Harris, *The Integration of Faith and Learning: A Worldview Approach* (Eugene, OR: Cascade Books, 2004), quoted in Mark P. Cosgrove, *Foundations of Christian Thought: Faith, Learning, and the Christian Worldview* (Grand Rapids, MI: Kregel, 2006), 19.

10. Geerhardus Vos, *Biblical Theology: Old and New Testaments* (Grand Rapids, MI: Eerdmans, 1948; reprint, Edinburgh: The Banner of Truth Trust, 1975), 9.

11. You could argue that a more basic "identity" category is that of image bearer. That is true, but because the Scriptures are God's revelation to his people (with obvious spillover into unbelievers' lives), I am using distinctions that would apply to Christians this side of Christ's return.

12. Remember the importance of studying these passages in their original context, which I do not have the space to do. I am highlighting

features of these texts that by "redemptive extension" are true for us today.

13. Notice how Peter uses Old Testament language/metaphors to describe Christians, which demonstrates the continuity between Israel and the church.

14. For a masterful discussion of how the cross transforms the sufferings of God's people, see Richard B. Gaffin Jr., "The Usefulness of the Cross," *Westminster Theological Journal* 41, no. 2 (Spring 1979): 228–46.

15. For a helpful book on the reality of indwelling sin, see Kris Lundgaard, *The Enemy Within: Straight Talk About the Power and Defeat of Sin* (Phillipsburg, NJ: P & R, 1998).

Chapter 6

1. I hope to give a feel for how to connect specific passages with specific issues of life later in the book. However, the use of Scripture in personal ministry does not always involve opening the Bible to a specific chapter and verse. Just as God communicates his truth in a variety of modes (genres), so the specific ways in which we minister the Word will vary.

2. A quick reading of your study Bible's introduction to Chronicles would give that overview.

3. Dan McCartney and Charles Clayton, *Let the Reader Understand: A Guide to Interpreting and Applying the Bible,* 2nd ed. (Phillipsburg, NJ: P & R, 2002), 123.

4. Al Wolters, *The Song of the Valiant Woman: Studies in the Interpretation of Proverbs 31:10–31* (Carlisle, UK: Paternoster Press, 2001), 74.

5. Consider Brian E. Daley, "Is Patristic Exegesis Still Usable? Some Reflections on Early Christian Interpretation of the Psalms" in *The Art of Reading Scripture,* eds. Ellen F. Davis and Richard B. Hays (Grand Rapids, MI: Eerdmans, 2003), 69–88.

6. To be fair, the early church fathers used allegory as only one approach to interpretation although they considered it important nonetheless.

7. Graeme Goldsworthy, *Preaching the Whole Bible as Christian Scripture* (Grand Rapids, MI: Eerdmans, 2000), ix.

Chapter 7

1. You might ask here, "Can you use these questions with nonbelievers?" It is true that the category of "saint" does not apply to those who are not Christians. In that case, it is better to think in terms of the broader

category, "image bearer." This person is a fallen image bearer but God's image bearer nonetheless. This means I approach the person with dignity and compassion. I may highlight the marks of God's "common grace" in his life, even as I urge him to submit the whole of his life to the One who is Creator and Redeemer. I use a God-shaped lens to reframe the good in his life as evidence of God's "kindness, tolerance and patience" that should lead to repentance (Rom. 2:4). Of course, these conversations usually evolve over time, as you build relationship.

2. See Michael R. Emlet, "Understanding the Influences on the Human Heart," *Journal of Biblical Counseling* 20, no. 2 (Winter 2002): 47–52, for further development of the ways in which these three influences impact our lives before God.

3. Paul David Tripp, *Instruments in the Redeemer's Hands: People in Need of Change Helping People in Need of Change* (Phillipsburg, NJ: P & R, 2002), 128–33.

4. Ibid., 127, emphasis original.

5. See David Powlison, "Idols of the Heart and 'Vanity Fair'" *Journal of Biblical Counseling* 13, no. 2 (Winter 1995): 35–50.

6. A more comprehensive set of questions can be found in David Powlison, "X-Ray Questions: Drawing Out the Whys and Wherefores of Human Behavior" *Journal of Biblical Counseling* 18, no. 1 (Fall 1999): 2–8.

7. Particularly helpful resources include Jeannine K. Brown, *Scripture as Communication: Introducing Biblical Hermeneutics* (Grand Rapids, MI: Baker Academic, 2007), and Dan McCartney and Charles Clayton, *Let the Reader Understand: A Guide to Interpreting and Applying the Bible,* 2nd ed. (Phillipsburg, NJ: P & R, 2002). I require both of these books in my Biblical Interpretation class. Also helpful and less technical are Tremper Longman III, *Reading the Bible with Heart and Mind* (Colorado Springs, CO: NavPress, 1997) and Daniel M. Doriani, *Getting the Message: A Plan for Interpreting and Applying the Bible* (Phillipsburg, NJ: P & R, 1996). Longman's book is particularly important for understanding how "genre" (the type of literature a particular passage is)—e.g., history, poetry, prophecy, and so on—affects interpretation and application. This is crucial for reading the Bible wisely, so I encourage you to use Longman's resource, particularly if you haven't had much instruction in biblical interpretation.

8. I do recommend buying introductions to both the Old Testament and the New Testament, which will greatly assist study of the original context. My picks include: Tremper Longman III and Raymond B. Dillard, *An Introduction to the Old Testament,* 2nd ed. (Grand Rapids, MI: Zondervan, 2006); D. A. Carson and Douglas J. Moo, *An Introduction to*

the New Testament, 2nd ed. (Grand Rapids, MI: Zondervan, 2005); and David deSilva, *An Introduction to the New Testament: Contexts, Methods, and Ministry Formation* (Downers Grove, IL: InterVarsity Press; Leicester, England: Apollos, 2004).

9. Realize, however, that you may not have many clues to the original historical situation that prompted the writing of the passage/book, particularly in the Old Testament. The pastoral-theological aims of a text may "fit" several different times in history. So, *firm* conclusions about how the passage impacted its first hearers/readers may not be possible, but doing this grammatical-historical spadework does equip you for further steps in the interpretive process.

10. See Dean Flemming, *Contextualization in the New Testament: Patterns for Theology and Mission* (Downers Grove, IL: InterVarsity Press, 2005).

11. Using drama as an overarching metaphor for approaching theology, Kevin Vanhoozer writes, "Christians may know their lines and have the right propositional knowledge, but a mere mental assent to information, by itself, stops short of having a decisive impact on our lives. It is not enough to parrot our lines; we have to *live our parts." (The Drama of Doctrine: A Canonical-Linguistic Approach to Christian Theology* [Louisville, KY: Westminster John Knox Press, 2005], 370, emphasis original.)

12. Alasdair MacIntyre, *After Virtue: A Study in Moral Theology,* 2nd ed. (Notre Dame, IN: University of Notre Dame Press, 1984), 216.

Chapter 8

1. These case studies are composites of several people.

Chapter 9

1. The ESV translates Haggai 2:7 as, "'And I will shake all nations, so that the treasures of all nations shall come in, and I will fill this house with glory, says the LORD of hosts.'"

2. You should also ask what other biblical books are set in the same time period because that will lend perspective and perhaps even help with chronology, as it did in this case. For example, Ezra 1—6 takes place in 537 BC, and Zechariah is a contemporary of Haggai.

3. The two study Bibles I'm most familiar with are the *Spirit of the Reformation Study Bible* (NIV) and *The Reformation Study Bible* (ESV); see bibliography.

4. The ESV renders Haggai 2:9 as, "The latter glory of this house shall be greater than the former. . . . " In this translation, it's not clear

whether the second temple will exceed Solomon's temple in glory or whether only the second temple is in view. That is, although it's a small start, this second temple will end up looking glorious. This highlights the importance of reading a passage in several translations, especially if you are doing more in-depth study. But either way, the main idea is that God has something more glorious planned for the future.

5. Leland Ryken, James C. Wilhoit, and Tremper Longman III, *Dictionary of Biblical Imagery* (Downers Grove, IL: InterVarsity Press, 1998).

6. Notice that in the span of one chapter (2 Chron. 6) Solomon speaks of God dwelling both in the temple (v. 2) and in heaven (v. 21). This seeming contradiction is resolved when you see that the temple was the connecting point between heaven and earth. The temple was the place where the God of heaven lived with his people on earth. See N. T. Wright, *Simply Christian: Why Christianity Makes Sense* (San Francisco: HarperSanFrancisco, 2006), 64–65. Psalm 11:4a holds both aspects together in one verse: "The LORD is in his holy temple; the LORD is on his heavenly throne."

7. Perhaps the visit of the Magi (Matt. 2:1–12) is a fulfillment of Haggai 2:7—the treasures of all nations coming to the true King!

8. One other helpful New Testament passage that furthers the temple imagery is Ephesians 2:19–22.

9. Eugene Peterson, "Living into God's Story," http://www.biblicaltheology.ca/blue_files/Living%20into%20God%27s%20Story.pdf (accessed Dec. 30, 2008).

10. I'm using "counselor" not simply in its more narrow, formal sense but also in its broader, informal sense. You might be Tom's friend, pastor, Bible study leader, elder, or formal counselor. You are someone who is simply trying to bring God's wisdom to bear on Tom's life in a proactive way.

11. In real life, I probably would not immediately move to a passage at this point but would explore Tom's last statement in more depth (e.g., in what ways does Sarah's response discourage him? How does he see this coming out in his attitude toward God, toward Sarah, and toward others? And so forth.)

12. This is really a personal extension of 1 Corinthians 3:16, where Paul describes the church (corporate) as the temple of the Holy Spirit.

13. See Stanley J. Grenz, *Prayer: The Cry for the Kingdom,* rev. ed. (Grand Rapids, MI: Eerdmans, 2005) for an extended treatment of the relationship between the coming of the kingdom and prayer.

Chapter 10

1. Remember, however, that Mark is writing his Gospel *after* the resurrection, which is important as you consider the potential purposes for this narrative. In other words, you need to consider how the message of Mark 1:40–45 relates to Mark's themes and purposes for his entire Gospel.

2. You could also ask, How does this connect with the thematic emphases for the Gospel of Mark as a whole? Where do you see the theme(s) of this passage elsewhere in Mark?

3. The same Greek word is translated as "good news" in Mark 1:15.

4. This detail is provided in the margin notes in most study Bibles. If you don't have such a Bible, checking a cross-reference or two would give the same information.

5. James R. Edwards calls it a "contagious holiness." *Mark, Pillar New Testament Commentary* (Grand Rapids, MI: Eerdmans, 2002), 70.

6. J. R. R. Tolkien, *The Return of the King,* part III, *The Lord of the Rings,* 2nd ed. (London: George Allen & Unwin Ltd., 1966), 134–47.

7. Ibid., 136.

8. Ibid., 138–39.

9. Ibid., 144.

10. This is the technical term New Testament scholars use for this command to secrecy given by Jesus.

11. This is not unlike Jesus' reply to John the Baptist when John hesitated to perform the baptism: "It is proper for us to do this to fulfill all righteousness" (Matt. 3:15).

12. Edwards, *Mark,* 72. Edwards in fact summarizes the passage as "Jesus Trades Places with a Leper," which underscores the reversal that takes place.

13. For a more substantial argument, see Robert H. Gundry, *Mark: A Commentary on His Apology for the Cross* (Grand Rapids, MI: Eerdmans, 1993). David deSilva notes, "What does Mark wish to say to his readers? Jesus' messiahship is not present in his power only but also in his suffering and death. His lordship is not merely in his exaltation to the right hand of God but in his service to others to the point of being lifted up on a cross. Indeed, his subsequent exaltation shows that Jesus' way is the way of true greatness and honor in the sight of God. God's ways are *not* human ways." (*An Introduction to the New Testament: Contexts, Methods, and Ministry Formation* [Downers Grove, IL: InterVarsity Press; Leicester, England: Apollos, 2004], 208, italics original.)

14. D. A. Carson and Douglas J. Moo, *An Introduction to the New Testament,* 2nd ed. (Grand Rapids, MI: Zondervan, 2005), 185–86. They go on to note that there are many other themes within Mark that do not so easily fall into these categories, which underscores my earlier point that

the emphases of a particular passage connect with, but not necessarily fully overlap, the themes and purposes for the book as a whole.

15. Because Jesus is "front and center" in Gospel passages, we are implicitly dealing with the question, "How does the writer portray the in-breaking of God's kingdom in Christ?" (chap. 7). But we will want to consider how other New Testament writers develop the themes of the passage.

16. Other related concepts/themes include purity, purification, sacrifice, cleanse, cleansing, holy/unholy, consecrate/consecration, and defile/defilement.

17. Jesus engages the Pharisees and teachers of the law on the issue of cleanness vs. uncleanness in Mark 7. There Jesus teaches that what ultimately makes a person unclean is not something external (e.g., dirty hands) but something internal: "Nothing outside a man can make him 'unclean' by going into him. Rather, it is what comes out of a man that makes him 'unclean'" (7:15). Jesus goes on to say in verses 20–23, "What comes out of a man is what makes him 'unclean.' For from within, out of men's hearts, come evil thoughts, sexual immorality, theft, murder, adultery, greed, malice, deceit, lewdness, envy, slander, arrogance and folly. All these evils come from inside and make a man 'unclean.'" You might say his teaching points to a deep, internal, spiritual uncleanness present in all people, which manifests itself in sinful thoughts and actions. Cleansing must occur at the heart level.

18. In a real-life situation, I probably would have pursued a further understanding of Tom's experience and view of God before opening to this (or another) passage. Again, this dialogue is "telescoped" for the sake of illustration.

19. Notice that I am urging Tom to imitate the leper's desperation and humility in coming to Jesus while not losing sight of Mark's focus on Jesus.

20. Joseph Hart, "Come, Ye Sinners, Poor and Wretched," 1759. *Trinity Hymnal,* rev. ed. (Norcross, GA: Great Commission Publications, 1990), hymn 472.

21. You could also consider 1 Peter 1:17–21: "Since you call on a Father who judges each man's work impartially, live your lives as strangers here in reverent fear. For you know that it was not with perishable things such as silver or gold that you were redeemed from the empty way of life handed down to you from your forefathers, but with the precious blood of Christ. . . ."

22. Tolkien, *The Return of the King,* 142.

23. Jesus called the healed leper to specific action as well—don't tell anyone and go, present the appropriate sacrifices—but he did not heed

Jesus' call. This side of the resurrection, however, no "gag rule" exists! We are meant to tell others about our cleansing and invite them to join us in relationship to Jesus.

24. In Luke 12, in the context of discussing worry over material security, Jesus says to the disciples, "But seek his kingdom, and these things [food, clothing, shelter] will be given to you as well. Do not be afraid, little flock, for your Father has been pleased to give you the kingdom" (vv. 31–32). If Jesus has given his disciples the kingdom, the possession of all possessions, why should we worry about material things? If God has given us his own Son, will he fail to give us everything else we really need? (Rom. 8:32). For an extended treatment of these themes, see David Powlison, "Don't Worry," *Journal of Biblical Counseling* 21, no. 2 (Winter 2003): 54–65.

25. Jesus highlights the importance of kingdom "deed" ministry in many places but the Parable of the Sheep and Goats (Matt. 25:31–46) is particularly striking.

Chapter 11

1. I hope that the examples of dialogue with Tom and Natalie went a long way in showing such balance is possible.

2. Even preaching and formal teaching, which tend to be more one-way communication, should spark ongoing conversations between believers. But the sheer "content" of what is shared in those public contexts is likely to be more than what occurs during a formal hour of counseling, let alone a more informal ministry encounter.

3. Biblical scholars call this the "hermeneutical spiral."

4. C. S. Lewis, *The Last Battle: The Chronicles of Narnia, Book 7* (New York: HarperCollins, 1994), 185.

5. In this sense, there is a "temporal" process to discovering the Christ-centered aspects of a text.

6. It is true that this application of Scripture *was* more implicitly Christ-centered than the Romans 12 passage because it referenced the resurrection.

7. Graeme Goldsworthy, *Preaching the Whole Bible as Christian Scripture* (Grand Rapids, MI: Eerdmans, 2000), 60–61.

8. George Eldon Ladd notes, "In the death and resurrection of Christ, the Old Testament promises of the messianic salvation have been fulfilled, but within the old age. The new has come within the framework of the old; but the new is destined also to transform the old" (*A Theology of the New Testament*, rev. ed. [Grand Rapids, MI: Eerdmans, 1993], 412). See also the helpful diagrams on pp. 66–67 that illustrate

this overlap of the ages. Again, I have been arguing that our use of Scripture must keep in mind *our* time and place in redemptive history—postresurrection, post-Pentecost, postclosing of the canon, pre-second coming of Jesus. Similarly, Edmund P. Clowney argued against "synagogue sermons"—preaching an Old Testament text and its application without connecting it to the redemptive work of Christ. ("Preaching Christ from All the Scriptures" in *The Preacher and Preaching: Reviving the Art in the Twentieth Century,* ed. Samuel T. Logan Jr. [Phillipsburg, NJ: P & R, 1986], 164.)

9. For a discussion of the already-and-not-yet character of our salvation, see Herman Ridderbos, *Paul: An Outline of His Theology* (Grand Rapids, MI: Eerdmans, 1975.) See also Romans 8:15–27 and Philippians 3:12–21, where the already-and-not-yet aspects of our redemption are evident.

10. See Edward T. Welch, *Running Scared: Fear, Worry, and the God of Rest* (Greensboro, NC: New Growth Press, 2007).

11. Not the least of which is because you yourself are transformed by an increasingly gospel-centered approach to the Scriptures!

12. Tod E. Bolsinger, *It Takes a Church to Raise a Christian: How the Community of God Transforms Lives* (Grand Rapids, MI: Brazos Press, 2004).

13. For a discussion of how the Lord's Supper forms us into the image of Christ, see Craig R. Higgins, "Spiritual Formation and the Lord's Supper: Remembering, Receiving, Sharing," *Journal of Biblical Counseling* 24, no. 3 (Summer 2006): 71–78.

14. Remember, even these "spontaneous" connections arise out of a previous familiarity with particular biblical passages or themes, often from in-depth study and meditation perhaps months or years earlier.

15. Remember what I said earlier in the book: getting a sense of the author's original pastoral intent suggests potential applications in the present day.

16. I first heard these stories given a gospel slant by Pastor John Hall, but I have adapted them more specifically for the use of Scripture in ministry.

Bibliography

Bartholomew, Craig G. and Michael W. Goheen. *The Drama of Scripture: Finding Our Place in the Biblical Story.* Grand Rapids, MI: Baker Academic, 2004.

Bauckham, Richard. "Reading Scripture as a Coherent Story." In *The Art of Reading Scripture,* edited by Ellen F. Davis and Richard B. Hays, 38–53. Grand Rapids, MI: Eerdmans, 2003.

Bolsinger, Tod E. *It Takes a Church to Raise a Christian: How the Community of God Transforms Lives.* Grand Rapids, MI: Brazos Press, 2004.

Brown, Jeannine K. *Scripture as Communication: Introducing Biblical Hermeneutics.* Grand Rapids, MI: Baker Academic, 2007.

Carson, D. A. and Douglas J. Moo. *An Introduction to the New Testament.* 2nd ed. Grand Rapids, MI: Zondervan, 2005.

Chapell, Bryan. *Christ-Centered Preaching: Redeeming the Expository Sermon.* 2nd ed. Grand Rapids, MI: Baker Academic, 2005.

Chapman, J. Wilbur. "Jesus! What a Friend for Sinners!" 1910. Hymn 498. *Trinity Hymnal.* Rev. ed. Norcross, GA: Great Commission Publications, 1990.

Clark, Jayne V. "Confronted by Anger." *Journal of Biblical Counseling* 24, no. 1 (Winter 2006): 6–13.

Clowney, Edmund P. "Preaching Christ from All the Scriptures." In *The Preacher and Preaching: Reviving the Art in the Twentieth Century,* edited by Samuel T. Logan Jr, 163–91. Phillipsburg, NJ: P & R, 1986.

————. *The Unfolding Mystery: Discovering Christ in the Old Testament.* Phillipsburg, NJ: P & R, 1988.

Daley, Brian E. "Is Patristic Exegesis Still Usable? Some Reflections on Early Christian Interpretation of the Psalms." In *The Art of Reading Scripture,* edited by Ellen F. Davis and Richard B. Hays, 69–88. Grand Rapids, MI: Eerdmans, 2003.

Davis, Ellen F. and Richard B. Hays, eds. *The Art of Reading Scripture.* Grand Rapids, MI: Eerdmans, 2003.

deSilva, David. *An Introduction to the New Testament: Contexts, Methods, and Ministry Formation.* Downers Grove, IL: InterVarsity Press; Leicester, England: Apollos, 2004.

Doriani, Daniel M. *Getting the Message: A Plan for Interpreting and Applying the Bible.* Phillipsburg, NJ: P & R, 1996.

————. *Putting the Truth to Work: The Theory and Practice of Biblical Application.* Phillipsburg, NJ: P & R, 2001.

Edwards, James R. *Mark. Pillar New Testament Commentary.* Grand Rapids, MI: Eerdmans, 2002.

Emlet, Michael R. "Understanding the Influences on the Human Heart." *Journal of Biblical Counseling* 20, no. 2 (Winter 2002): 47–52.

Enns, Peter. "Apostolic Hermeneutics and an Evangelical Doctrine of Scripture: Moving Beyond a Modernist Impasse." *Westminster Theological Journal* 65 (2003): 263–87.

————. *Exodus. The NIV Application Commentary.* Grand Rapids, MI: Zondervan, 2000.

Flemming, Dean. *Contextualization in the New Testament: Patterns for Theology and Mission.* Downers Grove, IL: InterVarsity Press, 2005.

Fowl, Stephen E. and L. Gregory Jones. *Reading in Communion: Scripture and Ethics in Christian Life.* Eugene, OR: Wipf and Stock, 1998.

Gaffin, Richard B., Jr. "The Usefulness of the Cross." *Westminster Theological Journal* 41, no. 2 (Spring 1979): 228–46.

Goldsworthy, Graeme. *Preaching the Whole Bible as Christian Scripture.* Grand Rapids, MI: Eerdmans, 2000.

————. *The Goldsworthy Trilogy: Gospel and Kingdom, Gospel and Wisdom, The Gospel in Revelation.* Carlisle, Cumbria: Paternoster Press, 2000.

Gorman, Michael J. *Cruciformity: Paul's Narrative Spirituality of the Cross.* Grand Rapids, MI: Eerdmans, 2001.

Green, Joel B. "The (Re-)Turn to Narrative." In *Narrative Reading, Narrative Preaching: Reuniting New Testament Interpretation and Proclamation,* edited by Joel B. Green and Michael Pasquarello III, 11–36. Grand Rapids, MI: Baker Academic, 2003.

Grenz, Stanley J. *Prayer: The Cry for the Kingdom.* Rev. ed. Grand Rapids, MI: Eerdmans, 2005.

Gundry, Robert H. *Mark: A Commentary on His Apology for the Cross.* Grand Rapids, MI: Eerdmans, 1993.

Harris, Richard A. *The Integration of Faith and Learning: A Worldview Approach.* Eugene, OR: Cascade Books, 2004. Quoted in Mark P. Cosgrove, *Foundations of Christian Thought: Faith, Learning, and the Christian Worldview.* Grand Rapids, MI: Kregel, 2006.

Hart, Joseph. "Come, Ye Sinners, Poor and Wretched" 1759. Hymn 472. *Trinity Hymnal.* Rev. ed. Norcross, GA: Great Commission Publications, 1990.

Hays, Richard B. *The Moral Vision of the New Testament: Community, Cross, New Creation; A Contemporary Introduction to New Testament Ethics.* San Francisco: HarperCollins, 1996.

Higgins, Craig R. "Spiritual Formation and the Lord's Supper: Remembering, Receiving, Sharing." *Journal of Biblical Counseling* 24, no. 3 (Summer 2006): 71–78.

Johnson, Eric L. *Foundations for Soul Care: A Christian Psychology Proposal.* Downers Grove, IL: InterVarsity Press, 2007.

Jones, L. Gregory. "Embodying Scripture in the Community of Faith." In *The Art of Reading Scripture,* edited by Ellen F. Davis and Richard B. Hays, 143–59. Grand Rapids, MI: Eerdmans, 2003.

Ladd, George Eldon. *A Theology of the New Testament.* Rev. ed. Grand Rapids, MI: Eerdmans, 1993.

Lane, Timothy S. and Paul David Tripp. *How People Change.* 2nd ed. Greensboro, NC: New Growth Press, 2008.

Lewis, C. S. *The Last Battle: The Chronicles of Narnia, Book 7.* New York: HarperCollins, 1994.

———. *The Voyage of the Dawn Treader: The Chronicles of Narnia, Book 5.* New York: HarperCollins, 1994.

———. *The Weight of Glory and Other Addresses.* New York: Touchstone/Simon & Schuster, 1996.

Longman, Tremper, III. *Reading the Bible with Heart and Mind.* Colorado Springs, CO: NavPress, 1997.

Longman, Tremper, III and Raymond B. Dillard. *An Introduction to the Old Testament.* 2nd ed. Grand Rapids, MI: Zondervan, 2006.

Lundgaard, Kris. *The Enemy Within: Straight Talk About the Power and Defeat of Sin.* Phillipsburg, NJ: P & R, 1998.

MacIntyre, Alasdair. *After Virtue: A Study in Moral Theology.* 2nd ed. Notre Dame, IN: University of Notre Dame Press, 1984.

McCartney, Dan G. "*Ecce Homo:* The Coming of the Kingdom as the Restoration of Human Vicegerency." *Westminster Theological Journal* 56 (1994): 1–21.

———. "The New Testament's Use of the Old Testament." In *Inerrancy and Hermeneutic,* edited by Harvie M. Conn, 101–16. Grand Rapids, MI: Baker, 1988.

McCartney, Dan and Charles Clayton. *Let the Reader Understand: A Guide to Interpreting and Applying the Bible.* 2nd ed. Phillipsburg, NJ: P & R, 2002.

Peterson, Eugene. *Eat This Book: A Conversation in the Art of Spiritual Reading.* Grand Rapids, MI: Eerdmans, 2006.

———. "Living into God's Story." http://www.biblicaltheology.ca/blue_files/Living%20into%20God%27s%20Story.pdf (accessed Dec. 30, 2008).

Powlison, David. "Counsel Ephesians." *Journal of Biblical Counseling* 17, no. 2 (Winter 1999): 2–11.

———. "Don't Worry" *Journal of Biblical Counseling* 21, no. 2 (Winter 2003): 54–65.

———. "Idols of the Heart and 'Vanity Fair.'" *Journal of Biblical Counseling* 13, no. 2 (Winter 1995): 35–50.

———. "The Practical Theology of Counseling." *Journal of Biblical Counseling* 25, no. 2 (Spring 2007): 2–4.

———. "X-Ray Questions: Drawing Out the Whys and Wherefores of Human Behavior." *Journal of Biblical Counseling* 18, no. 1 (Fall 1999): 2–8.

Pratt, Richard L., Jr., gen. ed. *Spirit of the Reformation Study Bible.* Grand Rapids, MI: Zondervan, 2003.

Ridderbos, Herman. *Paul: An Outline of His Theology.* Grand Rapids, MI: Eerdmans, 1975.

Robertson, O. Palmer. *The Christ of the Covenants.* Phillipsburg, NJ: P & R, 1980.

Ryken, Leland, James C. Wilhoit, and Tremper Longman III. *Dictionary of Biblical Imagery.* Downers Grove, IL: InterVarsity Press, 1998.

Sproul, R. C., gen. ed. *The Reformation Study Bible.* Lake Mary, FL: Lignonier Ministries, 2005.

Steinmetz, David. "Uncovering a Second Narrative: Detective Fiction and the Construction of Historical Method." In *The Art of Reading Scripture,* edited by Ellen F. Davis and Richard B. Hays, 54–68. Grand Rapids, MI: Eerdmans, 2003.

Tanner, Kathryn. "Scripture as Popular Text." *Modern Theology* 14, no. 2 (April 1998): 279–98.

The Scripture Project. "Nine Theses on the Interpretation of Scripture." In *The Art of Reading Scripture,* edited by Ellen F. Davis and Richard B. Hays, 1–5. Grand Rapids, MI: Eerdmans, 2003.

Tolkien, J. R. R. *The Return of the King.* Part III of *The Lord of the Rings.* 2nd ed. London: George Allen & Unwin Ltd., 1966.

Tripp, Paul David. *Instruments in the Redeemer's Hands: People in Need of Change Helping People in Need of Change.* Phillipsburg, NJ: P & R, 2002.

Vanhoozer, Kevin. *The Drama of Doctrine: A Canonical-Linguistic Approach to Christian Theology.* Louisville, KY: Westminster John Knox Press, 2005.

Vernick, Leslie. *How to Live Right When Your Life Goes Wrong.* Colorado Springs, CO: Waterbrook Press, 2003.

Vos, Geerhardus. *Biblical Theology: Old and New Testaments.* Grand Rapids, MI: Eerdmans, 1948. Reprint, Edinburgh: The Banner of Truth Trust, 1975.

Walsh, Brian J. and J. Richard Middleton. *The Transforming Vision: Shaping a Christian World View.* Downers Grove, IL: IVP, 1984.

Warfield, B. B. *The Inspiration and Authority of the Bible.* Phillipsburg, NJ: P & R, 1948.

Webb, William J. *Slaves, Homosexuals, and Women: Exploring the Hermeneutics of Cultural Analysis.* Downers Grove, IL: InterVarsity Press, 2001.

Welch, Edward T. *Running Scared: Fear, Worry, and the God of Rest.* Greensboro, NC: New Growth Press, 2007.

Williams, Michael. "Systematic Theology as a Biblical Discipline." http://www.biblicaltheology.ca/blue_files/Systematic%20 Theology.pdf (accessed Dec. 24, 2008).

Witherington, Ben III. *Paul's Narrative Thought World: The Tapestry of Tragedy and Triumph.* Louisville, KY: Westminster/John Knox Press, 1994.

Wolters, Albert M. *Creation Regained: Biblical Basis for a Reformational Worldview.* 2nd ed. Grand Rapids, MI: Eerdmans, 2005.

————. *The Song of the Valiant Woman: Studies in the Interpretation of Proverbs 31:10–31.* Carlisle, UK: Paternoster Press, 2001.

Wolterstorff, Nicholas. *Divine Discourse: Philosophical Reflections on the Claim That God Speaks.* Cambridge: Cambridge University Press, 1995.

Wright, Christopher J. H. *Knowing Jesus Through the Old Testament.* Downers Grove, IL: InterVarsity Press, 1992.

————. *Old Testament Ethics for the People of God.* Downers Grove, IL: InterVarsity Press, 2004.

————. *The Mission of God: Unlocking the Bible's Grand Narrative.* Downers Grove, IL: IVP Academic, 2006.

Wright, N. T. *Simply Christian: Why Christianity Makes Sense.* San Francisco: HarperSanFrancisco, 2006.

————. *The Challenge of Jesus: Rediscovering Who Jesus Was and Is.* Downers Grove, IL: InterVarsity Press, 1999.

————. *The Climax of the Covenant: Christ and the Law in Pauline Theology.* Minneapolis, MN: Fortress, 1993.

————. *The New Testament and the People of God.* Minneapolis, MN: Fortress Press, 1992.

————. *What St. Paul Really Said: Was Paul of Tarsus the Real Founder of Christianity?* Grand Rapids, MI: Eerdmans, 1997.

Index of Scripture

*These numbers indicate pages where only the book name is referenced.